THE ARAB COCOON

The Arab Cocoon:
Progress and Modernity
in
Arab Societies

TAREK HEGGY

VALLENTINE MITCHELL
LONDON • PORTLAND, OR

First published in 2010 by Vallentine Mitchell

Middlesex House	920 NE 58th Avenue, Suite 300
29/45 High Street, Edgware,	Portland, Oregon,
Middlesex HA8 7UU, UK	97213-3786, USA

www.vmbooks.com

British Library Cataloguing in Publication Data:

Hajji, Tariq Ahmad.
  The Arab cocoon : progress & modernity in the Arab world.
  1. National characteristics, Arab. 2. Arabs—Ethnic
  identity. 3. Ethnopsychology—Arab countries. 4. Arab
  countries—Foreign relations—20th century. 5. Arab
  countries—Foreign relations—21st century.
  I. Title
  155.8'4927-dc22

ISBN 978 0 85303 922 8 (cloth)
ISBN 978 0 85303 892 4 (paper)

Library of Congress Cataloging-in-Publication Data
A catalog record has been applied for

Printed by The Good News Press Ltd, Ongar, Essex

To the Arab intellectuals entirely isolated from reality, that is, the representatives of the majority of the so-called Arab intelligentsia, who fail to understand pluralism and particularity within diversity, as well as the sheer fact that on earth, today, we have one civilization and several cultures. Their exerted 'Don Quixote' efforts to defend the Arab cocoon (described in this book) would add nothing but further isolation, backwardness and darkness, let aside the incremental failure to join mankind's march of progress. To them, this book is dedicated.

Tarek Heggy

Contents

1

Introduction

The purpose of this chapter is to record some of the impressions that I formed a few years ago during one of my visits to the United States. On that occasion, I spent a month at the invitation of ten of the most famous universities in America, as well as of six prestigious research centres which specialized in Middle Eastern affairs. I was privileged to address over a thousand of the top American academics and experts concerned with the Middle East and studying its past, present and future from every angle of scientific research, especially in the field of social sciences. Here, then, are some lessons drawn from this trip: lessons that make one question the status of 'progress' in the Arabic-speaking societies. The essence of these lessons can be summarized in the following points.

1. DISINTEGRATED ARAB PRESENCE IN INFLUENTIAL WESTERN INSTITUTIONS

From my visits to more than ten of the Middle East research centres with the greatest impact on what can be called the kitchen of ideas, or think tanks, in which US policies and attitudes are formed, including centres that have for years been supplying the State Department and the White House with Middle East specialists such as Dennis Ross[1] and many others before him, I noticed that despite the presence in many of these centres of sizeable contingents of Arab, Indian, Turkish and Iranian scholars and top experts, the members of each group do not interact as parts of a whole, but act as individuals, isolated islands scattered in a vast sea. In stark contrast to the lack of cohesion among the Arabs working in these institutions is an almost palpable sense of community among their Jewish-American colleagues, who have forged strong professional and personal links with each other as well as with visiting Israeli scholars and pro-Israeli non-Jewish scholars. While the Arabs are fragmented and lack a higher aim transcending their individual personal aims, the members of the Jewish group operate in tandem as an integrated and synergistic team to attain well-defined short-, medium- and long-term goals. Their mastery of the language and idiom of the age, and the skilful use of the methodological tools of scientific research to further their common aim, their ability to speak to the world in which they are living in its own language, using its own cultural references and symbols, has enabled them to become an influential force capable, to a great extent, of shaping the basic orientations of the United States in all matters related to the Middle East.

This situation is seen by some as merely confirming the validity of the conspiracy theory to which they subscribe, but that is a simplistic explanation for a phenomenon which is the result, rather, of a well thought out and diligently applied programme of action, a strategic game plan whose application has met with very little resistance. A counter-plan to redress the balance of influence, so to speak, can only succeed through the concerted and sustained efforts of a team using modern research methods and speaking in the language of the age – requirements that are not met by most of the members of the Arab academic community in the United States, with the exception of a small minority made up largely of Israeli Arabs, that is, Palestinians who did not leave their towns after 1948. The other Arabs scattered in these universities and research centres would do well to emulate their example.

One of the most prominent Israeli Arabs is Haifa-born Dr Shibley Telhami,[2] who heads the Sadat Department in the University of Maryland and who has successfully mastered the rules of a game he plays with great skill to the advantage of the Arab side. Indeed, he is now a recognized Middle East expert whose opinion is sought by decision-makers in the United States. The Arabs need hundreds more of his calibre, but these are unfortunately in short supply.

The majority of Arabs working in these establishments are either concerned only with their own narrow interests, passive spectators of the wider world around them, or demagogues using the fiery language so popular in such throwbacks to the 1960s as the Al-Jazeera TV channel,[3] which is reviving the declamatory style adopted by Arab media, during a decade that must assume a large share of responsibility for developing an Arab mindset in which the lines of demarcation between reality and rhetoric are often blurred.

The phenomenon of a substantial yet unfelt – and ineffectual – Arab presence in American universities and research centres needs to be addressed, and who can do this better than the Arab League, which has the resources to study the phenomenon in depth, and lay down programmes by which to maximize the strategic potential of that presence.

However, it must under no circumstances embark on such a project as what Nizar Qabbani called 'the logic of fiddle and drum',⁺ that unnecessarily strident and unconvincing brand of demagogy that has distorted the image of the Arabs in the West and alienated public opinion. Indeed, Arabic-speaking societies can expect no sympathy as long as they continue to conduct their discourse with the outside world in the form of verbal battles fought with the weapon of demagogy which, to quote Nizar Qabbani once again, 'never killed a fly'.

2. THE ARAB–ISRAELI CONFLICT: AN OBSTACLE TO PEACE AND A STRONG INTERIOR

I spoke on the Arab–Israeli issue at such length that I will not even attempt to summarize here what I said. But the main message I tried to get across to the thousands who attended my lectures was a simple one: the sooner the protagonists reach a just and equitable solution which responds to the basic aspirations of the majority of their citizens, the sooner the region can close the page on its turbulent history and move on towards a brighter future in which it can concentrate on building strong, flourishing modern communities living in social peace. This applies not only to the Arab side but also to Israel, who, though providing its citizens with some kind of democratic mechanism, is far from being a civil society in the real sense of the word. A just peace is the only mechanism that will allow for the emergence of societies that, while retaining their distinctive identity and cultural specificity, can display all the attributes of a modern civil society in the political, economic and social spheres.

I also spoke of fundamentalism as one of the main enemies of civil society, noting that Jewish fundamentalism stood as a major obstacle in the way of a comprehensive Middle East peace. This greatly angered my audience, whose sensibilities were offended by an association that is not usually made in the West, where fundamentalism is rarely, if ever, spoken of in its Jewish dimension. The deliberate silence on the dangers of Jewish fundamentalism will remain unbroken as long as there is no one to address the issue in the language of the age and in the right forum, which is not the mosques of New Jersey and Los Angeles, but the main universities and research centres in America.

3. EDUCATION: ONE OF THE MAJOR ACHIEVEMENTS
OF HUMAN CIVILIZATION

I have long believed that before talking about educational reform in the generally accepted meaning of the term, which is the reform of the four pillars on which the institution of education rests (curricula, teachers, students, schools), one must first lay down the strategic aims of education in a policy paper – which need to be no longer than one page – and then design detailed programmes translating these aims into concrete procedures with regard to curricula, teachers, students and schools. I have also come to believe, in the last three years, in the existence of a direct connection between the strategic aims of education and the formation not only of modern citizens endowed with the qualities required to meet the challenges of the age, but also of a cadre of modern management leaderships, without which no society can make the required leap forward.

For it is now generally accepted that the driving force for an economic take-off which realizes social justice, creates new job opportunities, spreads a positive spirit in society in general and among the middle and lower-middle classes in particular, and preserves social peace while keeping abreast of the times – but without a loss of identity and cultural specificity – is a cadre of efficient executive managers, not academics or economists, although the expertise of these in their chosen field of specialization is, of course, indispensable.

As I see it, the institution of education is responsible not only for providing students with a reasonable level of knowledge in applied and social sciences, but also for instilling in them a set of fundamental values such as a respect for time, teamwork, perseverance and creativity, as well as the firm conviction that human beings are the most important resource for success and progress, that knowledge is universal, and, parallel to this, the importance of respecting their own identity (without falling into the trap of chauvinism), the spirit of competition; and a respect for pluralism.

A system in which the teacher is relegated to the role of a transmitter and the student to that of a receiver can only instil a spirit of apathy in its recipients, inhibiting any creative impulses they may have, reining in their imagination and stifling their intellectual curiosity and initiative. At best, it is a system capable of churning out traditional civil servants at a time when the demand for their services is on the wane. In this day and age, society does not require the public functionaries who were once indispensable cogs in the wheel on which society ran, but creative, competitive citizens who can function within the framework of a team and who, recognizing that knowledge is universal, seek to acquire knowledge from any source that can help them hone their competitive edge. These sources include:

1. The formation of a cadre of modern executive managers to lead economic life in the context of a new world order based on competition, whether globalization remains as ferocious as it now is or becomes a tamer process in future, which I believe to be more likely.
2. The formation of dynamic citizens eager to participate in public life and to expand the margin of democracy.
3. The formation of citizens at peace with themselves and with others, both within their own communities and in other communities, instead of the disgruntled citizens who are becoming all too common in the Arabic-speaking societies, who try to solve their problems with the sword of Jihad[5] rather than with the weapons of the age, namely through competition, hard work, creativity and keeping pace with the scientific and cultural achievements of human civilization.

These were just reflections on one of my visits to America, notes jotted down to record impressions before they fade with the passage of time.[6] My lectures elicited reactions ranging from enthusiasm to outrage. A particularly heated debate followed a lecture in which I spoke of the fact that the United States was a great power with a remarkably superficial culture, and the dangers this posed for the 'humanization' of such notions as democracy, human rights and accepting the 'Other'. The following chapters will elaborate on this last sentence, discussing the mentioned values of human civilization, and examining the role of the West – particularly of the United States – in promoting (or not) these values. The book will also explore the values of progress as the natural path of human civilization, and the problematic with these values of the Arabic-speaking societies.

NOTES

1. (Born 1948). American author and political figure; he played a major role in the involvement of the US in the Middle East under Republican President George H.W. Bush, and then Democratic President Bill Clinton.
2. (Born in 1951). American professor of political science; born near Haifa (Israel) in an Arab family of peacemakers; expert on US policy n the Middle East, and former advisor to the US Mission to the United Nations and the Iraq Study Group.
3. Arabic satellite TV based in Doha, Qatar.
4. (1923–98). Qabbani is a famous Syrian poet who abandoned his diplomatic career to focus on

writing poetry. His literary works consisted of two dozen volumes of poetry and regular articles in the Arabic-language newspaper *Al Hayat*. He was revered by generations of Arabs for his sensual and romantic verse, in which it seemed that women were his main theme and inspiration.

5.   Struggle 'in the way of God'.

6.   A more exhaustive account of the lectures, debates and round-table discussions with which the visit was filled will be given, as previously mentioned, in a book scheduled to appear shortly and which will reproduce the full texts of more than ten lectures I gave, and the discussions that followed each one.

2

Civilization: A Product of Human Values

Although the term 'civilization' crops up frequently in public discourse, not much effort is expended on trying to define what the term really means. It is often used as a byword for the model of the developed Western lifestyle which some of us seek to emulate. In fact, any civilization is in its essence nothing more than a collection of values. How a society regards its citizenry, the value it places on the individual and on personal freedom, the way in which it determines his/her relative position vis-à-vis the executive branch of government; whether it casts its rulers in the role of masters over or servants of the citizenry; the status and rights enjoyed by women, and by children; the value it places on time, on work, on the quality of work; its attitude to its minorities; the right of others to differ in beliefs, doctrines, opinions and behaviour – these are the values that form the fabric of civilization.

Some may be exalted and sublime, others degenerate and ignoble, but it is extremely important when looking at other civilizations to distinguish between two levels. At the local level, each civilization has features that are characteristic of it alone. But there is also a dimension of every civilization that is not exclusive to it but belongs to the mainstream of human civilization. For example, much of what constitutes 'Western civilization' is, in fact, the product of the accumulated experience of human civilization, whether in the fields of applied sciences or human and social sciences. The most striking example of a civilization where the two levels have merged in close-to-perfect harmony is Japan.

Here the Arabs must rethink the enmity and hatred that some of them harbour for Western civilization, on the grounds that it is an alien civilization. Actually, many of its most exalted values are the fruit of mainstream human civilization. Blind enmity to developed civilizations is a rejection of the essence, lessons, wisdom and accomplishments of the collective human experience, not to mention a reflection of ignorance, narrow-mindedness and fanaticism.

There are none more misguided than those who call for the adoption of the applied scientific and technological achievements of the West and the rejection of all other aspects of Western civilization. The essence of human civilization extends beyond the fields of applied science and technology, to philosophy, art, literature, human rights and other fields. Some of the Arabs reject Western civilization without realizing that they are rejecting elements of human civilization, to which they, like others, have made many contributions. This enmity stems from a deep ignorance of the fact that Islam extols most of the fundamental principles on which developed civilizations are based. Likewise, much of what they believe to be the basic principles of their civilization are no more than adaptations and embodiments of regressive and degenerate values that first emerged in the Dark Ages, in the years of tyranny, repression and ignorance. Indeed, many did not emanate from Islam but from cultures in the context of which Islamic history unfolded and from which it acquired inferior values.

The phenomenal economic success of Asia's newly industrialized countries (NIC) only confirms how important it is to distinguish between noble cultural values, on the one hand – many of which the Arabic-speaking societies should adopt from the West – and aberrant, regressive values (wrongly ascribed by some to Arab cultural heritage), on the other – which they should discard.

1. THE HUMAN INPUT

Every writer concerned with history, politics and, especially, philosophy has a topic of particular interest. For example, the eminent historian Arnold Toynbee devoted much of his life to the study of why civilizations rise and fall. An exponent of the theory of cycles, he believed the universal driving force of progress to be the response to challenges. The eleventh-century Islamic theologian, mystic and philosopher Abu Hamid Muhammad al-Ghazali,[1] known as 'hujjat al Islam' (the proof of Islam), journeyed across the Muslim world driven by the desire to find out whether the human senses could attain knowledge of the existence of God. Meanwhile, Nietzsche's[2] world outlook was pervaded by his 'caste of masters' theory, the belief in an ever-progressing elite up to the level of 'superman';[3] and Karl Marx,[4] who was and remains a philosopher before being a theoretician of economics, politics and sociology, had an all-encompassing philosophy based on his view of the dynamics of history, which stemmed from his basic ideas on the relation of matter (the infrastructure) to ideas (the superstructure).

One of the most dominant figures of contemporary Arab thought, Abbas al-Aqqad,[5] focused on his fundamental idea that exceptional human beings are the driving force of human civilization, and history in general. Many of Aqqad's disciples, and I am among them, have been saddled with the arduous task of researching the role of the individual in shaping human history. Anyone undertaking this line of research is bound eventually to find him/herself at the crossroads of major philosophical and political paths. He/she must then choose between them, difficult as this may be. Every single philosophical, political, economic and social school of thought has its own views on the matter, based on its carefully predicated tenets. I believe that extensive and careful readings for years can bring the reader to the first step on the path to a clear answer. Philosophical schools of thought, in general, are divided into idealistic, or moralistic, schools on the one hand, and materialistic schools on the other. All the answers to the major questions concerning the role of the individual in shaping history are also divided into two types of answers, one departing from idealistic philosophical premises, the other, in one way or another, from materialistic philosophical premises.

The Dialectical Materialists (the disciples of Karl Marx who, like the German philosopher Ludwig Feuerbach[6] before them, discarded the idealistic content of Hegel's philosophy of idealistic-dialectics[7]) firmly maintain that the role of the individual and of heroes and eminent men in shaping history is a minimal one. They believe that human history is propelled by a purely material driving force, the class struggle, which is the inevitable result of the interplay of the forces and relations of production prevailing at a given time. As for heroes and eminent men, they are like puppets dancing to the tune written by the supreme composer: the class struggle.

All historians who believe in a materialistic interpretation of history hold that it is socio-economic conditions that govern the movement of history, and that these purely materialistic considerations also determine the role of the individual. Hence their view, for example, that when the age of slavery came to an end, it was because changes in the forces of production and relations of production tipped in favour of the slaves, bringing slavery to an end and heralding in the age of feudalism. Similarly, purely material factors brought feudalism to an end and introduced capitalism. This third socio-economic formation, according to the materialists, was the result of the development of the forces of production. It was this development – culminating in the invention of the steam engine – that rang the curtain down on one phase of human history and ushered in a new one.

Such momentous events as the French Revolution are also

explained in purely materialistic terms by these exponents of the materialist school of thought, who dismiss the role of the individual and the
impact of the presence of certain figures on the scene of historic events
as being of little relevance. That is also the way they interpret the wars
and revolutions of the nineteenth century, as well as the birth of nationalist movements in Europe, under the leadership of Mazzini[8] in Italy
and Bismarck[9] in Germany. It is also the principle guiding their interpretation of Europe's colonialist expansion and the major events of the
twentieth century, such as the Russian Revolution of February 1917;
the Bolshevik takeover in October/November that same year under
Lenin's leadership;[10] the First World War; the rise of the Third Reich;
the Second World War; and all the national liberation movements in
Africa, Asia and Latin America.

The materialist interpretation of history could appeal to the scien-
tifically-minded reader because it is surrounded by an aura of science
and because of the rigour of its methodology. Without drawing the
reader into the eddies of the philosophical battle between 'matter' and
'thought', I will say only that I, for one, believe that the history of
mankind, indeed, life itself, is governed by an absolute, transcendental
Idea, and that to think that matter alone is the mover does not stand to
reason. In fact, the changes attributed by materialist determinists to
matter alone are in fact changes brought about purely by 'thought'.
The invention of the steam engine, for example, was not the result of a
materialist evolution; it was the result of intellectual evolution. From
the beginning of recorded history up to the present time, certain individuals have played a major role in shaping events. They have left an
indelible mark on our world and, had they not existed, events would
have taken a different course. A superficial look that does not go
beyond major historical events to analyse the personalities, characteristics and motivations of certain historical figures could lead one to
deny the role of such individuals in influencing the course of history,
and to believe that the major waves of history were governed only by
materialist factors. Such a view is totally refuted by the weight of such
historical figures as Alexander the Great,[11] without whom much of the
history of the ancient world would have been different. And, had it not
been for person of Napoleon Bonaparte,[12] the history of France and of
Europe would have followed a course different from the one we know
in the ten years following the French Revolution (1789–98). That the
reins of the Russian Revolution slipped from the hands of the
Mensheviks[13] nine months after they had overturned Tsar Nicolas II[14]
in February 1917 is due to the determining role of the man whom the

Germans helped return to Petrograd, via Zurich, in a special military train, for they believed in his ability to change the situation in Russia. That man was Lenin[15] who, in a matter of months, signed the Brest–Litovsk treaty by virtue of which the Germans obtained what they wanted of him.[16]

Had it not been for the role played by Adolph Hitler,[17] the events of the 1930s and 1940s on the European scene and in the world at large would not have been the same, for they were the result of Hitler's 'actions' and the 'reactions' of his enemies, the Allies, led first by Britain and, towards the end, by the United States.

2. THE HAND OF DESTINY

To give but a few examples:

If Corsica had not been annexed by France at a given point in time and had remained a part of Italy, Napoleon[18] would not have been born French and would not have come to play the crucial role he played in the history of France, of Europe and of many other parts of the world, ever since his star began to rise during the last five years of the eighteenth century until his ultimate fall in 1815.

The personal role of King Henry VIII[19] drove thousands of Englishmen into Protestantism, a fact which greatly influenced the climate of political and public life in Britain.

Had it not been for the personal role of Gamal Abdel Nasser,[20] internal events in Egypt, relations between Egypt and the Arab world and between the Arab states and Israel would have taken a completely different course.

If it had not been for the role played by a handful of men during the last third of the nineteenth century and the first third of the twentieth, the Zionist movement would not have gone as far as it has done in the last forty years. It is thanks to the role played by one man – Lee Kuan Yew, prime minister of Singapore since 1965 – that such a small country managed to develop so dramatically in just two decades.

All the above implies neither a negation of the role and impact of socio-economic or material factors on history, nor a belief that history is made up of a series of consecutive events that, like soap operas, are not governed by some rule or system. What it does say is that the two factors combined both have a role to play: the material factor as the general trend, as well as the non-material factor – or the role of individuals and circumstances – having an equally important role with the same impact as that of the material factor.

Two references come to mind here: *The Heroes* by Plutarch[21] and *Heroes and Hero Worship* by Thomas Carlyle.[22] These brilliant works, together with Toynbee's extensive twelve-volume-study of history,[23] can clearly show the reader who wishes to pursue the subject further, the effect of the two factors combined on the course of human history, with the predominance of the moral factor, as represented by the role of particular individuals, ideas and circumstances.

3. THE FRUITS OF THE CIVILIZED MARCH OF MANKIND

In a lecture I delivered in February 2001 at Princeton University, I pointed out that what some call 'Western civilization' is not purely Western but the culmination of a number of civilizations that flourished at different historical moments. Like tributaries feeding a river, these civilizations – Egyptian, Chinese, Sumerian, Phoenician, Greek, Roman and Arab – merged together to form the mighty river of human civilization. At the same time, I conceded that the present stretch of the river, in which the civilizing process has attained its highest level ever, owes many of its features to its geographical location, which is the West. Thus it is a product of human endeavour through the ages in some respects, while in others it is purely Western, although its greatest achievements in the areas of artistic, literary and intellectual creativity owe more to the collective human experience than they do to its purely Western dimension.

To study the ancient Egyptian civilization in depth, especially the aspect dealing with conscience and ethics (which inspired the famed Egyptologist and orientalist James Henry Breasted to call Egypt the 'Dawn of Conscience', not only the cradle of civilization); or the role of Sumerian civilization in laying down legal and legislative frameworks and developing humankind's idea of God (first propounded by the Chaldean prophet Abraham), or the aspect of Chinese civilization dealing with values; or the rich contributions made by the philosophers of Ancient Greece and, before them, of Hellenistic Egypt; or the work of Averroes and the early Renaissance philosophers, is to realize that human civilization is an integral whole, a continuum of human endeavour that has flowed in an unbroken stream through the ages. To my mind, human civilization has more to do with ethics and values than with monuments and scientific achievements; its greatest accomplishments are represented not in the awesome scientific and technological advances made in the fields of medicine, space and the information revolution, but in the following:

1. Democracy.
2. General freedoms.
3. Human rights.
4. Respect for 'Otherness'.
5. The expanding frontiers of communication and links between people at all levels through a process that some call globalization which, in its present unbridled form, appears to be driven by purely economic considerations without sufficient regard to the humanitarian dimension. I believe this is bound to change and that globalization with a more human face is not far off.
6. The development of education in line with the requirements of the age, so that in many societies it has come to serve wide segments of the population and not only a limited elite.

This is not to say, however, that these six great achievements of human civilization have come to full fruition, or even that they are any-where near maturity. Unfortunately, they are still only localized (that is, present in some places and not in others), characterized by duality (that is, double standards) or regarded by some as applicable only to them and not to others. This state of affairs reflects a certain uncivi-lized – not to say barbaric – way of thinking which is based on reasons rooted in history and known to any student of Western civilization, particularly one familiar with the effect that the Anglo-Saxon (Viking)[24] component has had on its development. The legacy of this component takes its most extreme form in what I call the 'cowboy cul-ture'. But this, in and of itself, does not explain why the six values have not yet come into their own at the global level. Other factors, some internal, some external, conspired to impede their development during the last hundred years, and make them accessible to some and not to others.

The following chapter will examine the consequences of the Second World War as factors obstructing the development of the achievements of human civilization.

NOTES

1. (1058–1111). Persian Orthodox Ash'arite theologian.
2. (1844–1900). German philosopher and philologist; he questioned the value and objectivity of truth; his influence remains in existentialism and postmodernism.
3. Übermensch, see Nietsche's book *Thus Spoke Zarathustra* (Chemnitz: Ernst Schmeitzner 1883–85).
4. (1818–83). Prussian revolutionary philosopher and political economist, author of *The Communist Manifesto* (1848).
5. (1889–1964). Largely self-educated Egyptian writer, historian, poet, philosopher, translator and journalist.

6. (1804–72). German philosopher.
7. (1770–1831). German philosopher Georg Wilhelm Friedrich Hegel. See his book *The Science of Logic*, published in Germany in 1811, 1812 and 1816 (revised 1831).
8. (1805–72). Giuseppe Mazzini was an Italian philosopher and politician; he played a major role in creating modern Italy.
9. (1815–98). Otto von Bismarck was minister-president of Prussia as well as chancellor of the North German Confederation. He was responsible for the unification of Germany in 1871.
10. (1870–1924). Vladimir Ilyich Ulianov, aka Lenin, was a Russian communist politician; he was the leader of the October Revolution which overthrew the Russian Provisional Government, which had followed the abdication of Tsar Nicholas II (1917) (see note 14 below). Lenin was the first head of the Russian Soviet Socialist Republic (1917), then of the Soviet Union (1922).
11. (356–323 BC). Ancient Greek king; reputed military commander; his empire was extended by his conquests in the East and South; founder of the city of Alexandria (Egypt) which was named after him.
12. (1769–1821). Corsican Emperor of France; renowned for his military skills, he conquered several European countries; he had a strong impact on the history of Europe. Much of what is known about Ancient Egypt today is owed to his expedition to Egypt (1798) which included more than 160 scientists.
13. A faction of the Russian revolutionary movement; they emerged in 1903 after a dispute with Lenin's followers (see note 10) who are known as the 'Bolsheviks'.
14. (1868–1918). Tsar of Russia, king of Poland, and grand duke of Finland; his ruling started in 1894, but he had to abdicate in 1917 for failing to control the Russian Revolution. He is also known as 'Saint Nicholas the Passion Bearer' (Russian Orthodox Church).
15. See note 10.
16. Treaty which made the Russians surrender the Ukraine, Finland, the Baltic Provinces, the Caucasus and Poland to Germany and Austro-Hungary in 1918.
17. (1889–1945). Austrian-born, German leader of the Nazi Party and Chancellor of Germany (1933–45); he is the perpetrator of the Holocaust, which is known to have caused the death of about six million Jews.
18. See note 12.
19. (1491–1547). King of England and lord (then king) of Ireland; he separated the Anglican Church from the Authority of Rome; this opened the doors to the emergence of Protestantism against the Catholic Church.
20. Jamal Abdel-Nasser (1918–70). Second Egyptian president 1954–70. Graduated from the Military Academy in 1938. Participated as battalion commander in the 1948 War between the Arabs and the fledging State of Israel. After the war, he organized the Free Officers group, which consisted mainly of low-ranking officers, mostly from humble backgrounds, whose objective was to revamp what was believed to be a corrupt system (implying the ousting of the then-called royal dynasty). On 23 July 1952 they successfully executed a coup. Initially the officers installed coup leader General Mohamed Naguib as president. After growing dissent and rivalry, Nasser ousted Naguib and became the official president in 1954. Under his leadership Egypt underwent a series of economic, social and political reforms. He banned all parties except his own Arab Socialist Union. In the economic sphere he pursued a socialist policy, nationalizing in 1961 all major industries and utilities and adopting an ambitious development plan, with the project of the Great Dam of Aswan being one of his main achievements. His regime also carried out agrarian reform, redistributing agrarian lands in Egypt. In the international and inter-Arab sphere he adopted a nationalistic revolutionary Arab policy and was one of the co-founders of the non-alignment bloc in 1955. During his time in office, Egypt's foreign policy tilted towards the Soviet Union and the Eastern bloc. Some of his most salient actions in the international arena were the nationalization of the Suez Canal in 1956, the union with Syria, the Egyptian involvement in Yemen and the 1967 War, after which he resigned for twenty-four hours only to be reinstated following popular clamour. After his death, Nasser was succeeded by Anwar Al-Sadat.
21. (46–120). Greco-Roman historian and philosopher.
22. (1795–1881). Influential Scottish historian of the Victorian era.
23. (1852–83). English economic historian; he worked on the improvement of the social and economic conditions of the working classes.
24. Having Scandinavian influence; renowned for toughness and ruthlessness.

3

The Cold War Era (1945–90)

1. THE RISE OF THE COLD WAR

On 1 September 1939, the Second World War broke out.[1] It was a conflict that can be described as the greatest in the history of humanity. The war erupted between two sides; on one side were the Axis powers, which included Nazi Germany, fascist Italy and dictatorial Japan. Those three countries did not believe in democracy as it was defined by Western countries such as Britain, France, the Scandinavian states and the USA. On the other side of the war were the Allied powers. It can be said that the Allied group was categorically inharmonious. In addition to democratic countries – according to the Western definition – such as the US and Britain, it also included the Soviet Union, which was a dictatorial regime in the fullest sense of the word. The Soviet government described itself as a dictatorial, proletarian regime. The Second World War ended with the destruction of the triangle of the Axis camp, Italy, Germany and finally Japan, which surrendered when two atomic bombs were dropped on the cities of Hiroshima and Nagasaki in August 1945.[2]

The end of Second World War, however, was the beginning of another large-scale conflict, which has been described as the Cold War. Since the Soviet Union had joined the Allied camp, it was difficult for the rest of the Allies to turn their backs on their wartime communist partner and start a traditional war against the Soviet Union, which was an extremely essential ally despite being completely contradictory, politically as well as economically.

As soon as the Second World War ended, 'yesterday's Allies' became 'today's enemies'. The US, Britain and countries from what was later to be called Western Europe found themselves in confrontation with their former ally, the Soviet Union – a country which, following the war, was becoming larger, more powerful and more influential.

I would like to concentrate on describing the world scene at the end of the Second World War, because this particular situation is the source of the two historical paths or options which will be discussed in this chapter. Before the Second World War broke out in 1939, the Soviet Union was contained within its borders, although it had patriarchal relations with other communist movements worldwide through an organization that the Soviets established to support such movements, and which was called Communist International or the 'Comintern'.

The military defeat of Germany and Japan created a power vacuum in the international arena after the Second World War. In Europe, the German army began withdrawing westward after it had reached the gateway to Stalingrad. Simply speaking, as the German army retreated from east to west, the Soviet army occupied the territory that the German army abandoned. At first, the Soviet forces moved forward within their own territory, then they advanced into other countries that later formed the Warsaw Pact and the 'Comecon'[3] and were known as the Eastern European countries or the countries beyond the Iron Curtain. Consequently, all the lands that were removed from the realm of German sovereignty became new areas of influence for the Soviet Union and its political and economical ideologies. As a result of the German retreat to the west, the bloc of countries in Eastern Europe was formed, and those countries became like planets orbiting around the Soviet Union.

A similar process took place in Asia. When the Japanese army retreated from the vast territories that it had conquered outside of the Japanese home islands, communist parties in those areas took over the evacuated lands.

Although this process took place in more than one country, there are numerous examples, including Korea, Vietnam, Laos, Cambodia and Mongolia;[4] the greatest and the most important case in point was that of Mao Tse-tung in China.[5] He, and after him the remnants of his communist followers, proceeded to replace the withdrawing Japanese forces; simultaneously they swept away the Chinese anti-communist alternative led by Chiang Kai-shek,[6] who withdrew from the Chinese mainland and settled on the island of Formosa.[7] For years, the Western world considered the exiles on Formosa to be the official Chinese representatives, and dismissed the great giant mainland with its population exceeding one billion people.

Thus, the so-called free world came out of the Second World War victorious over its enemies, but the gains of the Soviet Union were bigger and far more important than those of its allies in the war.

The Second World War ended but the Cold War began and continued until the announcement of the dissolution of the Soviet Union in 1991. During the years from 1945 until 1991, the controlling factor in international politics was the conflict between the two poles of the Cold War.

2. THE CONSEQUENCES OF THE COLD WAR

A. USA Supremacy

It is noteworthy that when the Second World War broke out in September 1939, the United States adopted a neutral stance despite the efforts made by Britain's wartime prime minister, Winston Churchill,[8] to drag it in on the side of the Allies.[9] The United States only entered the war in December 1941, following the Japanese attack on its naval base in Pearl Harbor.[10] US industrial and military power provided the Allies with the main strength necessary to stem the tide of initial Axis[11] successes in Europe and the Far East and, finally, to bring the war to a victorious conclusion in the summer of 1945. Although its intervention was the decisive factor in the Allied victory, the United States did not capitalize on this fact in the immediate aftermath of the war, but delayed calling in its debt for just less than half a century. In the logic of power politics, the US should have reaped the fruits of the victory it was instrumental in achieving right after the war ended, but fate intervened in the form of the Cold War, which began in 1945 and lasted until 1991. During that period, the United States was locked in a battle for global supremacy with the Soviet Union, which stood as a formidable obstacle between the United States and its dream of unchallenged domination of the post-war world order. With the collapse of the Soviet Union and its satellite states, the moment for which the United States had been waiting since 1945 finally arrived. It was now free to stake its claim to global leadership on the strength not only of its victory in both the Second World War and the Cold War, but also of its uncontested political, economic, scientific and military superiority.

The emergence of the United States as the unique superpower on the world stage, which had been delayed by the Cold War, was further delayed by Bill Clinton's accession to power in January 1993. Under his administration, America held back from asserting its new international status (which reflected the post-Cold War balance of power) too blatantly. However, I believe that if the first president Bush had won a second term in the November 1992 presidential elections, the world would have seen then what it has been seeing since the Republicans regained power in January 2001. For the group of right-wing conservatives at the helm of the Republican Party are more direct when it comes to dealing with the realities of power than anyone else in America.

During the Cold War, the contrast between the value system prevailing inside American society and certain aspects of its foreign policy was disconcerting to outside observers. On the domestic front, America upheld values that had helped make it one of the most advanced societies in the world in all fields. It could rightfully claim an impressive level of democracy, a rate of economic productivity higher than one quarter of the entire global productivity, a vibrant culture, pre-eminence in the fields of science, technology and research and the strongest military force in the world. But America did not uphold the same values when it came to its dealings with the outside world. Justifying its actions as dictated by the conditions of the Cold War, American foreign policy had no qualms about maintaining friendly relations with corrupt and despotic military juntas in Central and South America, as well as with equally unsavoury regimes in Africa and Asia. It also supported and used radical forces with extremist views, including groups, organizations and countries it now regards as enemies.

One of the most important results of the Cold War culture is that US foreign policy lost sight of the fact that democracy is not only a human right for all the peoples of the world (including those of the Middle East), but that it is also the only safety valve than can protect humanity from the scourges of despotism, totalitarianism and extremism. During the Cold War, the United States was occasionally concerned with upholding democracy and human rights and with combating despotism and corruption outside its own borders, but only when it served its interests to do so. However, it turned a blind eye to blatant human rights violations and glaring manifestations of corruption perpetrated by friendly regimes or those with which it had interests in common. A deep crisis is facing many countries today because the United States has suddenly taken it upon itself to introduce democracy, by force if necessary, into societies which it was content for many years to leave at the mercy of corrupt and tyrannical rulers, whose subjects were brainwashed into believing that national pride entailed standing up to the challenge of Western civilization.

America's newly assertive stance as the unchallenged custodian of world order has not been met with universal favour. Not everyone is willing to accept that the new situation is an inevitable result of the seismic shift in the global balance of power. There are those who dispute the right of the United States to lay down the political and economic rules governing our world today, and others who question whether expressions like 'sovereignty' and 'international legitimacy' still have any meaning. Moreover, a number of incidents in 2008 (mostly reinforced by extremely high oil prices) made some think (or even dream) that the USA supremacy era is fading away. A view that I strongly believe will fade away (the view, not the USA supremacy!).

B. Korea: Two Choices, Two Results

In spite of the fact that the Cold War can be considered from many perspectives, this part of the chapter will concentrate on only one issue, namely the division between the two Koreas. The specific reason behind choosing the Korean issue is my belief that it summarizes most of the facts, the characteristics and the repercussions of the Cold War era.

The major players of the Eastern camp during the Cold War have, since 1991, categorically changed their political, economic and social policies. The Soviet Union, all of the Eastern European countries except Belarus, all the Asian socialist countries except North Korea, and the entire socialist Third World except Cuba have redefined their political and economical policies. Neither Belarus nor Cuba represent and exemplify the Cold War era as the two Koreas did and are still doing.

Korea was one nation before being divided by the ideologies of the Cold War era. The people of the two Koreas are racially the same, and they speak the same language. The greatest distinguishing feature between the two Koreas emerged due to disparate choices between two historical paths and destinies. Therefore, forty-five years after the end of the Korean War, it is the right of the reader to know, and the duty of writers on the subject to explain, the reasons that led to the creation of two Koreas. There is a South Korea that moves, works and lives politically and economically in concurrence with the Western system, and a North Korea which circled in the orbit of the Eastern bloc, strictly speaking of Mao Tse-tung's communist China.

Thus, humanity has the ability to see, reflect on and examine the repercussions of each path, and the respective choices of South Korea and North Korea. In my belief, these two choices are the most significant characteristics of the era of the Cold War. Equally, the modern results of the two significant historical choices of each Korea represent the fruit and consequence of each choice.

When more than half a century ago the Korean Peninsula was divided into two nations – North and South Korea – the number of people living in each of the states was almost the same. Today, due to the deteriorating living and health conditions and the high mortality rate among children in North Korea, its population numbers only half that of South Korea's 50 million.

It is noteworthy that while the mortality rate among children in South Korea is six in every thousand, in North Korea the percentage is four times more than that. This means that in North Korea, twenty-four children out of every thousand newborns die before their first birthday.

I think it is appropriate, for the benefit of the message of this chapter, to offer readers a number of significant comparative facts that I have compiled during a prolonged study of the two countries.

For example, while the number of telephone lines in South Korea reaches 24 million, in North Korea there are less than two million telephone lines. The annual electrical consumption for the whole of South Korea is 320 billion kWh, while North Korean state consumes only 21 billion kWh annually, which means that the amount of electricity being used in South Korea is fifteen times greater than that used in North Korea. Furthermore, while South Korea consumes 650, 000 barrels of oil on a daily basis, North Korea consumes only 25,000 barrels. In other words, South Korea's usage of petrol is 2,500 per cent higher than North Korea's. It is worthy of mention that there is a certain mathematical relationship between the amount of petrol used in any society and the level of economical development in that society. The greatest proof for this equation is China. While the Chinese economy has been growing at a rate of 9 per cent annually, there has been a consummate increase in the country's demand for petrol and other fossil fuels.

In addition to the previously mentioned comparisons between the two countries, the amount of the total economic production in South Korea is equivalent to $1,200 billion, while the economic production in North Korea does not exceed $40 billion, which means that the local production of South Korea is thirty times what it is in North Korea. The per capita real income in South Korea has reached $24,000 per year, while in North Korea it is less than $1,800 per year. It could be useful and even funny for readers to know that the average height of males in South Korea has increased to 1.74 m, while it remains 1.58 m among North Korean males. Finally, life expectancy in South Korea is approaching 80 years, while it is less than 70 in North Korea.

I think that readers will agree that these comparative statistics are extremely significant indicators that need no explanation. One country chose poverty, backwardness, and suffering, while the other chose progress, prosperity, health, and production. In terms of the pride of a nation, one side chose to receive donations and financial aid, while the other chose development and wealth and has subsequently obtained excess funds so that it can offer aid to others. In other words, one Korea chose to follow the Western model, the other chose the Eastern one which proved to be one of the major obstacles to the development of human values.

This was just one example of the divisions caused by the Cold War which emerged as an outcome of the Second World War, and which had its share of responsibility in obstructing the march of civilization. More impediments to this march will be explored in the next chapter.

NOTES

1. A war which involved most of the world, mainly opposing England, France and the former Soviet Republics (later joined by the USA) to Germany, Italy and Japan (1939–45).
2. The bombings which were ordered by US President Harry S. Truman killed about 220,000 people.
3. 'The Council for Mutual Economic Assistance'.
4. Countries of East Asia.
5. (1893–1976). Prominent Chinese military leader, head of the Communist Party of China and leader of the People's Republic of China since it was established in 1949 until his death in 1976. He is one of the most influential political figures in modern history.
6. (1887–1975). Chairman of the National Military Council of the Nationalist Government of the Republic of China from 1928 to 1948. He failed to eradicate the Chinese Communists, and had to retreat to Taiwan where he died as the president of the Republic of China.
7. The main island of Taiwan.
8. British prime minister from 1940 to 1945 and from 1951 to 1955.
9. Britain, France, US, USSR, Australia, Belgium, Brazil, Canada, China, Denmark, Greece, Netherlands, New Zealand, Norway, Poland, South Africa, Yugoslavia.
10. An unexpected attack launched by the Japanese navy against the US naval base (Pearl Harbor) in Hawaii in 1941, during the Second World War.
11. Germany, Italy, Japan, Hungary, Romania, Bulgaria.

4

The Hurdles Impeding 'The Civilized March of Mankind'

As explained in the previous chapter, the Cold War had negative effects on the development of human civilization. This chapter will look more deeply into the obstacles resulting from the Cold War.

1. MARXISM

The most important external factor impeding the development of civilization was the scourge of Marxism, which originated in the West but spread out to afflict many societies in different parts of the world. Without exception, these societies found themselves sidelined in the march of human civilization as a result of their failure to promote and develop the six notions described in Chapter 2. Moreover, the collapse of Marxism shifted the leadership of Western civilization away from the point at which a certain balance existed between power and culture (or power and knowledge) to a new focal point where information took precedence over knowledge (the acquisition of information and the acquisition of knowledge being two entirely different things).

For someone such as myself, who closely followed the literature and experience of Marxism for many years, and has written three critical books on the subject,[1] it is clear that Marxism is a purely European product born in a purely European environment. European conditions in the nineteenth century are what produced Marxism, and any attempt to depict it as a superstructural theory of history is not only completely off the mark, but is also in open contradiction with the fundamental Hegelian laws[2] upon the basis of which the edifice of Marxism was constructed. This view of Marxism as the product of a specific time and place is shared by numerous scholars who have proved the existence of an organic link between nineteenth-century Europe and Marxist thinking. Given that the soil in which it took root has changed virtually beyond recognition, the demise of Marxism 107 years after the death of its brilliant founder (Karl Marx died in 1883, Marxism in 1990) should have come as no surprise.

There is a great deal of evidence establishing the link between conditions in nineteenth-century Europe and Marxism but I will cite only one here, namely Friedrich Engels' groundbreaking book, *The Conditions of the Working Class in England* (1845), arguably the most influential text in the development of Marxist thinking. Not only does this stand as positive proof that the conditions which prevailed in Europe during the nineteenth century are what spawned Marxism, but it also helps explain why, with the disappearance of the specific features which led to its emergence, the scourge of Marxism which had for long afflicted Western civilization was bound to disappear too. It must be said, however, that it has disappeared more completely from the countries of Europe than it has from those of the Third World. There are objective reasons for this, reasons that must be understood and respected – if not necessarily condoned.

In short, it can be said that in its search for social justice, Marxism rode roughshod over the six values which I consider to be the greatest achievements of human civilization (when Western influence was predominant); as a theory of social and economic organization designed to further the welfare of people, it should have rather consecrated and reinforced those values.

Society versus the Individual

People whose intellectual and social outlooks were shaped by the ideas of Karl Marx view the 'individual' and 'society' very differently from those whose perceptions were shaped by the value systems in Western democracies. Where Marxists and, indeed, all socialists play down the role and importance of the individual and magnify the role and importance of society, in Western democracies the reverse is usually the case. Without delving into details, it is clear that developments on the world stage over the last twenty-five years have vindicated the exponents of the latter school of thought.

Socialists believe in society with a capital 'S', predicating all their systems on the assumption that a transcendental entity called society exists of and by itself, and that the primary function of government and the economic system is to serve it. Liberals, in contrast, do not believe in society as a mutually exclusive entity, but in a community of individual citizens who are collectively known as society. The individual is a tangible entity, society is not. Thus, a prosperous and successful society is nothing more than an aggregate of prosperous, successful citizens. By the same token, a society plagued with problems is also the sum total of its parts: unsuccessful citizens combatting a range of problems and deprived of the ability to work create the manner in which public life is conducted.

In Western democracies such basic concepts as human rights, the principle of legitimacy, freedom of thought and speech, and so on, all aim at adopting the fundamentals of democratic states focusing on changing individual citizens. This is the key to transforming society. I would go as far as to maintain that society is merely a term coined to refer to average individuals and the common values, trends, attitudes and circumstances they share. To my mind, bringing about a positive change in individuals is the task of those holding the keys to the political, economic, cultural and social machinery of society – in other words, of government, in the broad sense of the word.

While it may be true that modern management sciences did not exist in the days when Karl Marx formulated his all-encompassing theoretical manifesto, today these sciences have become the main driving force of contemporary developed societies. They are the locomotive which allows developed societies to forge far ahead of their underdeveloped counterparts, leaving them to limp along, or, in some cases, to grind to a complete standstill. Among the main principles of modern management sciences are those pertaining to human resources and quality management, which are based on the assumption that human beings are the most valuable resource for production, progress and prosperity. Indeed, human resources management is the determining factor in the progress or decline of any given organization, company, institution or people.

The temple of socialism has come crashing down, and socialist ideology and experience are buried in the rubble. Standing on the ruins will only perpetuate failure and establish a pattern of crises and disasters. The ability to differentiate between the ideas stemming from the barren wasteland of socialism and those beckoning to the fertile gardens of success, production and prosperity is the key to differentiating between illusion and reality when it comes to choosing the right options.

It is worth noting that some people who should have been among the first to embrace the cardinal principles of the new age, despite their professional ability and competence, continue to cling to principles and value systems that have no place in today's world. The only explanation for this blind loyalty to socialist ideals (or, in some cases, to the notion of state capitalism) by people who should know better is that it reflects a certain nostalgia for their youth in the 1950s or 1960s.

Thus, one can only admire the Chinese for avoiding this pitfall and for their accomplishments in recent years. When the leaders of the People's Republic realized that socialist ideas had become obsolete, they decided to open the economy to market forces, thereby giving an enormous boost to China's gross national product. However, they did not open the door to ideological debate because they understood that this would only sharpen differences and bring about a damaging schism between past, present and future.

2. THE WESTERN 'FAUX-PAS'

The second serious obstacle standing in the way of the six values is the fact that global leadership today has devolved to the United States of America, which is culturally the weakest link in the Western chain. Despite its awesome material power, superior scientific prowess and undeniable accomplishments in the field of communications and information technology, it remains the poorest member of the club of Western civilization in terms of culture and knowledge, its elites easily distinguishable from their counterparts in other Western societies by the shallowness of their cultural formation, the paucity of their knowledge and a tendency to confuse information with knowledge. I believe it is this that makes millions of intellectuals in the Third World sceptical of the United States' calls for democracy and human rights. In addition to the cultural poverty of the American government and people, the United States displays a degree of raw pragmatism that would put Niccolo Machiavelli[3] to shame.

Defined as a doctrine that both truth and conduct are to be judged by practical consequences, pragmatism places interests before moral considerations. America's pragmatic worldview is the result of the supremacy of might in the absence of culture, in addition to the Viking ingredient in its make-up.[4] Although it attempts to sugar-coat the realities of naked power by invoking moral considerations to explain its actions, its blatant use of double standards disqualifies it from its self-appointed role as the moral policeman of the world.

No one can dispute the importance of democracy, general freedoms, human rights, respect for 'Otherness', removal of barriers between nations and societies, and education based on promoting initiative and creativity rather than on teaching by rote. Sadly, there is a huge gap between the words of the main proponent of these values and its deeds, which are marked by double standards and determined solely by immediate economic interests, even if the fulfilment of those interests entails trampling the values underfoot. There is a clear absence of a

cultural dimension in most of the United States' orientations and decisions, which display a racism lurking not far beneath its shining surface.
Indeed, I believe there is a not inconsiderable theocratic dimension
behind the civilized secular facade presented to the world. All of which
makes attempts by the United States to market these principles an
exceedingly difficult task.

A. *The Lack of Rounded Knowledge*

I will refer once again to the month I spent lecturing at some of the most
important universities and Middle East research centres in the United
States. During my tour, I found an impressive wealth of 'information' on
the Middle East but, although my lectures were attended by hundreds
of university professors and postgraduate students, I did not come across
a single person who could be described as a 'Renaissance man', like those
who can be found in the universities of Britain, France, Germany and
Italy. What I did find, rather, were researchers drowning in a sea of information but lacking a humanistic cultural formation based on a wide-
ranging knowledge of the great classics of human creativity.

Not surprisingly, this lack of cultural depth has caused America to
commit monumental blunders, such as when it threw all its weight
behind the theocratic movement in Iran during the 1960s in a misguided bid to counterbalance the Marxist Toudeh Party. When it realized – too late – that its policy had backfired, it switched gears and
adopted the exact opposite policy. So too with Afghanistan, where at
one time America supported forces that have since brought the country to the brink of ruin. Examples of the US blithely ignoring the
moral imperatives that purportedly shape its foreign policy abound,
from Zaire in Africa to the banana republics of Latin America,[5] to its
backing of medieval regimes in more than one continent (a prime
example of the moral ambivalence in which much of the United States'
actions are shrouded is the story of its relationship with Omar Abdel
Rahman).[6]

B. *The Dilemma of the Controversy Between Short-Term and Long-Term Interests*

A lively debate on how US foreign policy is impacting on the rest of the
world was engaged in by the participants at a symposium held on the
Atlantic coast in Abidjan a few years ago, which was attended by prominent members of the international political and cultural communities.
The debate centred on trying to find a rational explanation for the support the United States has been extending, since the end of the Second
World War up to the present day, to a large number of corrupt regimes

in the Third World, with often disastrous consequences. Indeed, it was thanks to American backing that many otherwise defunct regimes survived as long as they did, including those of several banana republics in South America, the Shah of Iran[7] and other unpopular rulers. In addition to consistently placing its bets on the losing side, the United States pursued a policy throughout the Cold War of supporting fundamentalist-theocratic-political movements in the belief that they could serve as a bulwark against the spread of communism.

What Washington failed to take into account is that once a genie has been let out of the bottle, there is no way it can be induced into going back in and that, moreover, the impact of its emergence in the light cannot be predicted with any degree of accuracy. It is widely understood that the Iranian revolution, which was to cause the United States a great deal of aggravation, was assiduously courted by Washington in the early days, before Khomeini[8] fled first to Iraq, and from there to France, which took him under its wing and away from the American embrace. But far from learning its lesson, the United States continued playing the theocratic card in a number of other cases to counterbalance the communist threat, which it regarded as a greater evil.

Perhaps the most famous illustration of how this irresponsible game can get out of hand is what happened in Egypt in the early 1970s, when the theocratic genie was used to offset the influence of the socialist genie which had been let loose in the 1960s. By the end of the decade, the theocratic genie had become strong enough to turn against the man who had been instrumental in giving it a new lease of life, Anwar Sadat,[9] who was assassinated by a member of Egypt's fundamentalist movement. Moreover, there is no doubt in my mind that the Palestinian theocratic genie was let out of the bottle in order to clip the wings of the secular Palestinian resistance movement, Fattah – an act of folly its perpetrators will rue for many years to come.

Participants at the Abidjan symposium spent many hours trying to come up with a logical explanation for this bizarre aspect of US foreign policy which, despite an abysmal record of failures, continues to be applied to this day. The theme of the debate was dictated by the venue of the symposium, Africa, where corrupt, despotic rulers kept in power by the United States have wreaked havoc on the peoples of the continent. Examples abound, but perhaps the most notorious was Zaire's Mobuto. My interpretation of the phenomenon differed from that of the other participants, some of whom attributed it to America's inexperience in the field of foreign affairs, others to Jewish domination over the American decision-making process.

My view was, rather, that American foreign policy is influenced by two sets of considerations. One set is related to its long-term interests, which dictate that the political system of the United States supports forces capable of moving their societies forward, in terms of both democratic development and economic growth; the other, running parallel with the first, is related to the short-term interests of powerful economic institutions, interests which are not necessarily compatible with those of the United States in the long term. The history of the United States since the end of the Second World War has been shaped by a constant tug of war between the two sets of considerations. Sometimes the decision-making process is more responsive to the short-term interests of economic institutions, leading to the disastrous alliances spoken of earlier; much less frequently, it operates to serve America's own long-term interests. When that happens, the United States astounds the world by taking principled stands in defence of legitimate rights, as when President Eisenhower[10] condemned the tripartite aggression against Egypt in 1956.[11]

If scientific socialism died because it carried within it the seeds of its own destruction, as represented in its inability to achieve economic success, so too does the so-called 'Free World', which is currently led by the United States, carry the seeds of its own destruction, in the form of the sharp discrepancy between the short-term interests that often determine its political decisions on the one hand and the long-term interests of its own society and those of the world at large on the other.

C. A Double-Edged Weapon

While these questions and reservations deserve serious tackling, and in spite of much criticism concerning 'Western leadership', there is another set of questions that the Arab mind ought to endeavour to answer, far from its historic love for 'big words' that are mostly entirely isolated from reality:

1. Is the policy of resistance against the West, defiance and confrontation a means to an end or an end in itself? If the latter, what are its material repercussions? And if it is a means, what are its chances of achieving the end to which it aspires?
2. Does a society's rejection of reform, development and modernization imposed on it by others reflect its understandable resistance to foreign interference, or does it reflect a rejection of those processes in absolute terms? Can any society avoid the imposition of reform,

development and modernization by external forces without that same society initiating such processes itself in response to the aspirations and needs of its own people, rather than in compliance with the demands of foreign powers?

3. In the early 1990s, a country in the region raised the slogan of 'development without change'. Although developing without changing is a contradiction in terms, none of the Arab intellectuals bothered to question what the slogan meant or to look into the reasons behind their culture's opposition to change in any sphere: political, economic, management, social, cultural, educational or mass media.

The 'refuseniks' can be divided into four groups. One group is made of diehard members of the various socialist camps. The second is made of so-called Islamic fundamentalists, who are in reality a medieval political party using religion as an attractive shield behind which to hide their real intent, much as Judaism was used by secular Jews to promote the Zionist project. The third is made of those whose animosity to Western civilization in general and to the United States in particular stems not from a socialist or fundamentalist ideology, but from their deep frustration at the failure of both the Arab renaissance movement and the pan-Arab project. The members of this group are firmly convinced that this is a direct result of a Western conspiracy against them, rather than of any intrinsic weakness in the structure of their own societies. As to the fourth group, it is made of the proponents of civil society.

The rejection of the six values mentioned earlier[12] by the first three groups attests to a shared fascist dimension which characterizes all those who believe that their ideological construct represents a universal truth, a closed system that has attained perfection as opposed to the flawed model of Western civilization. Actually, a perfect model of human civilization has yet to be invented, but at least Western civilization admits that it is flawed and has a long way to go before the six values to which it subscribes are fully developed. The members of the first three groups reject the six values on the grounds that they oppose their main exponents (the West in general and the United States in particular). This only confirms their fascist leanings, in that they do not offer a better alternative to these great human accomplishments, make no distinction between the values themselves and their main advocates and, finally, are not nearly as vociferous in their condemnation of negative features in their own societies as they are when it comes to

rejecting the United States' advocacy of these values on the grounds
that its policies are marred by double standards, opportunism and the
subjugation of principles to self-interest.

Only the members of the fourth group recognize that these values
do in fact represent the highest achievements of human civilization,
but this does not prevent them from seeing that the negative aspects of
the West in general and the United States in particular are reflected in
the practical application of those values at the human level. At the same
time, however, they see that internal factors in their own societies are
also preventing the values from realizing their full potential as a universal frame of reference valid for the whole of humankind. The most
important of these internal factors is the absence, or very limited presence, of general freedoms and democracy, the lack of any meaningful
social mobility and the political and financial corruption pervading
most Third World societies.

I am all for directing the harshest possible criticism at Western civilization, both in its Euro-centrist phase and its current American
phase, in order to show up the absence of a humanistic and rational
dimension in the West's advocacy of the six principles it considers the
cornerstone of its own civilization and the greatest achievements of
human civilization as a whole. But I believe that the Third World writers and academics who are most sharply critical of Western civilization
are motivated not by a desire to expand the scope of application of
these values to encompass the whole of humanity, but by the determination to maintain a status quo that is totally out of synch with modernity, progress, the onward march of civilization and fundamental
human aspirations. The systems they are trying to keep in place are not
in the least concerned with promoting these six values into rights to be
enjoyed by all the members of the human family, rather than exclusively by those belonging to Western civilization. This is borne out
most strongly by the fact that while they do not call for these values,
they also turn a blind eye to the countless violations of these principles
in their own societies.

It is thus important to make a distinction between those who are
critical of the West in general and the United States in particular for
not practising what they preach and not extending the application of
the noble principles they advocate beyond themselves to encompass
the whole of humanity, and those whose criticism is driven by altogether different motives. The latter group is determined to keep conditions as they are in the Third World, that is, totally divorced from the
six values that are the proudest achievements of human civilization.

Some of the members of this group who are most sharply critical of the model of Western civilization put their criticism to work for the account of alternative models that are inimical to progress, science, civilization and humanity. These alternatives have set their societies on a backward course, either to the Middle Ages or to the totalitarianism that destroyed entire generations in many countries, generations that lived and died without benefiting from these principles in any way. Totalitarian systems worked to the advantage of a handful of despotic tyrants and a circle of close associates who ruled in the name of an abstract entity known as 'the people', an amorphous mass that existed only in the rousing speeches to which such systems are prone, while in reality the people consisted of wretched individuals deprived of the most basic human rights and constantly told how lucky they were to be fed, educated, employed and housed!

If Arabs want to move from generalities to practical mechanisms, they must find an answer to the all-important question of how they can keep their faith in the intrinsic value and majesty of the six principles separate from their view of the West in general, and of the United States in particular, as false prophets of the principles they claim to uphold. To embrace the principles wholeheartedly while condemning the hypocrisy, double standards and Machiavellian self-interest that mark much of the behaviour of their main exponents is not easy, but the distinction must be made. The answer lies in the promotion and greater empowerment of civil society institutions, not only to guarantee that the distinction continues to be made, but also to keep the Arabic-speaking societies from falling into the hands of forces whose leaders claim to be the representatives of absolute Truth. Society can only protect itself from the malevolent impact of these forces on the dynamics of public life by working tirelessly to develop the institutions of civil society. For civil society has an undeniable interest in the propagation of these six principles and in protecting society from the forces of darkness, totalitarianism and backwardness. It also has an undeniable interest in preserving the positive aspects of the cultural specificity and identity of the Arabic-speaking societies.

D. The Policies of the US versus the Third World Future

There are all the more grounds for optimism thanks to the technological and information revolution which could help engender a general climate favourable to the positive development of human rights and environmental protection systems, which are still primitive, uncoordinated and extremely inequitable. In such a climate, long-term considerations that have for long been subsumed to the short-term considerations of special-interest groups with an inordinately powerful influence on the political decision-making process will come into their own.

A number of key states in the Third World can play an important role in fostering a climate conducive to just such a development. A necessary if not sufficient condition here is to defuse whatever tensions poison their relations with the United States at the present time. Maintaining these tensions will only reinforce the status quo, and leave the field open to short-sighted, short-term interests, with all what this implies for the prospects of global peace and stability. If these interests are given a free rein, they will be like a cankerous sore on the global body politic, eating away at the foundations of world order and paving the way to clashes, bottlenecks and explosions that could destroy the present world order, and bring the stage crashing down on the heads of its principal players.

A noted French professor of political science at Université de Paris I, summing up the conclusions reached by the debate of the Abidjan symposium, said: 'In other words, it is only if the United States discards the theory that these strange regimes are the only barrier in the face of global chaos that this worst-case scenario can be averted. By clinging to that theory, the United States is trying to avoid the breakdown of world order through methods that will only hasten its coming!'

DIALOGUE IS THE SOLUTION

Can anything be done to change this bleak picture? The answer lies in one word: dialogue. The Arabs have a responsibility to establish an effective presence in the American arena and to use the tools of the age, as others do, to make a sustained and cumulative effort (in concert with Europe, which enjoys a balance between power and culture) aimed at saving the train of civilization from being derailed by a reckless driver blinded by his own power and cultural myopia. But whatever reservations one might have about how the United States has comported itself since it became a great power after 1945 and the sole superpower after 1990, that is no reason to deny that the six values it advocates represent the greatest achievements of human civilization. Those who refuse to recognize this can best be described by the Arabic proverb as 'using truth to conceal a dishonest purpose'.

Not only are these six values the greatest achievements, but they are also the utmost and inseparable companions in the march towards the progress of humanity.

NOTES

1. These books – *Afqar Marxia fi al mizan* (Marxist Ideas in Balance), 1978; *Al sheyou'eya wal adian* (Communism and Religion), 1980; *Tajribati ma'al marxia* (My Experience with Marxism), 1983, and the English book, *Critique of Marxism*, 1992, retitled 'The Imperative Fall of Socialism' in its 2009 edition – were described in a review that appeared recently in a famous American newspaper as a critique of Marxism using Marxist philosophical tools.
2. Set by German philosopher Georg Wilhelm Friedrich Hegel (see Chapter 2, note 7).
3. (1469–1527). Italian diplomat, politician, philosopher, musician and poet; central political figure of the Renaissance era; his treatise *The Prince* showed ruthlessness in his realistic political theory.
4. See Chapter 2, note 30.
5. A term used to describe a number of South America's republics that were, for decades, headed by tyrannical military governments and were mainly generating income from the exportation of bananas to the world in general and to the USA in particular.
6. (Born 1938). Leader of the Egyptian terrorist 'Islamic Group (Al Gama'a al Islamiya)'.
7. (1919–80). Mohamed Reza Pahlavi was the monarch of Iran from 1941 until his demise by the Iranian Revolution in 1979.
8. (1902–89). Iranian religious scholar; leader of the Iranian Revolution which overthrew the Shah in 1979.
9. (1918–81). Egyptian president from 1970 to 1981. Graduated from the Military Academy in 1938. Expelled from the army and imprisoned in the 1940s for subversive political activities and suspicion of participation in plots to assassinate senior political figures. When he was released he rejoined the armed forces in 1950. He took part in the 1952 Free Officers Revolution and was a close ally of Gamal Abd-Al Nasser, who appointed Sadat in 1969 as his vice-president. When Nasser died, in September 1970, Sadat succeeded him as president. During the first years of his presidency, Sadat quelled leftist opposition, surprised Israel in what was considered the victory of the 1973 War and reoriented Egyptian foreign policy towards the West (especially towards the USA), reversing its long pro-Soviet inclination. He introduced a series of economic and political reforms, promoting liberalization. In 1977, in a dramatic act and as a gesture demonstrating his will for peace, Sadat flew to Jerusalem and addressed the Israeli Knesset (parliament). The culmination of the process initiated by his visit was the signing of an Egyptian–Israeli peace agreement at Camp David. In his last years in power, Sadat's rule suffered from growing disillusionment and opposition (mainly from Islamic elements), manifested in the popular riots that broke out in 1977 and his assassination, during a victory parade, on 6 October 1981 by Islamic militants belonging to the Jihad group.
10. (1890–1969). President of the United States from 1953 to 1961. He oversaw the ceasefire in the Korean War. Being a military man, he gave priority to nuclear weapons as defence; he also reinforced pressure on the USSR during the Cold War.
11. The coordinated attack on Egypt by Israel, Britain and France in October/November 1956, in which Israel occupied the Egyptian-controlled Gaza Strip and the Sinai Peninsula, and Britain and France landed ground troops in the Suez Canal area. The parties were forced to withdraw and cease all action because of heavy UN pressure and US and Soviet intervention. The attack followed a period of mounting tension between the parties, during which Egypt's new regime nationalized the Suez Canal Company and was perceived as threatening other interests of the former colonial powers of the region. The tension between Egypt and Israel originated in the 1954 Egyptian-imposed blockade on Israeli navigation in the Gulf of Aqaba (Eilat) and the cross-border infiltration and sabotage raids into Israel by Palestinian guerrillas (*fidaiyyin*), for which Israel held Egypt responsible. As a result of the war, Egypt consolidated its control of the Suez Canal, Israel's navigation rights in the Gulf of Aqaba were guaranteed, and a special UN force, the UNEF (United Nations Emergency Force), was created and stationed in the Sinai to patrol the Egyptian–Israeli border.
12. See Chapter 2, section 3.

5

Progress: An Outcome of the Civilized March

1. WHAT IS PROGRESS?

My interest in the issue of progress, which has preoccupied me for close on a quarter of a century, grew from my experience as a member of the international corporation to which I gave twenty years of my professional life. During those years, I saw the practical translation of progress in every aspect of the work environment, at both the organizational and operational levels. Thanks to a highly proficient workforce, the corporation's annual profits exceeded the national incomes of all the Arab countries combined. For two decades, I saw the ultimate expression of human progress unfold in the context of a highly sophisticated system of work based essentially on optimizing the use of human resources. My interest in the subject was not limited to a fascination with its day to day manifestations in the workplace; in an attempt to better understand the process itself, I embarked on a study of the dynamics, values and mechanisms of progress. In the last few years, the issue came to occupy the forefront of my concerns, and I set down some of my thoughts on the subject in a book entitled *The Values of Progress* (Dar el-Ma'aref, 2001). The book, which does not purport to be an exhaustive treatise on progress, addresses only one aspect of this supremely important feature of our contemporary world.

In the book, I tried to establish the following:

1. That progress is the product of a value system, not of a society's material wealth or natural resources.
2. That the value system which promotes progress is a product of the collective human experience, and does not derive exclusively from the European or American experience. The greatest proof of this can be found in the qualitative leap forward made by a number of East Asian societies when they adopted this system, which allowed them to achieve a level of progress commensurate with that enjoyed by advanced societies in the West.
3. That a society's adoption of the values conducive to progress does not negate or destroy that society's cultural specificity. Again, the

greatest proof of this lies in the experience of the East Asian societies, which adopted this system without in any way abandoning or detracting from their cultural specificity.

4. That the values of progress have evolved out of the cumulative legacy of various civilizations, even if the greatest contribution to their development and dissemination in modern times has undoubtedly been made by Western civilization.

5. That the values of progress include, but are not limited to, the following:
   - Value of time.
   - A culture of systems, not individuals.
   - Quality control or compliance with standards of performance.
   - A critical mind that accepts criticism and engages in self-criticism.
   - A belief in pluralism as a basic feature of life, knowledge, ideas and systems.
   - Modern management techniques or contemporary values of work (such as teamwork, human resource management, delegation, marketing and modern management mechanisms).

The Twin of Evolution

A closer look at the values of progress presented in the previous section shows that, despite the different characteristics of human civilizations, ancient and new, they are values that belong to the whole of humanity, to the march of human civilization in general, rather than to any specific civilization. As civilizations rose and fell, humanity was moving steadily ahead on a course that transcended the fortunes of this or that civilization. Thus, human history proceeded along two parallel courses simultaneously: the march of civilization, and the evolution of humanity; the values of progress owe their existence more to the latter than to the former. The failure to recognize that humanity is higher and more sublime than any civilization can only lead to racism and fanaticism. There is no disputing the fact that every civilization has drawn on the cumulative experiences of other contemporary or earlier civilizations, and woven them into the fabric of its own culture complex.

Given the undeniable existence of a common fund of human experience – a 'cumulative legacy', as it were – built up through the ages in such fields as mathematics and other applied sciences, how is this common legacy assimilated into human consciousness which is the repository of values? If we admit that much of modern mathematics came from Ancient Greece, that modern music owes much to Aristotle and that

the Latin–Germanic law-makers based their codification on the principles propounded in the Roman Justinian Code, and if a great
Egyptologist like James Henry Breasted found an undeniable link
between the highest contemporary value systems and those in force in
Ancient Egypt which he called the 'Dawn of Conscience', then we cannot fail to see that as culture ranks below civilization, civilization ranks
below humanity.

Students of history will find that all civilizations, whether ancient or
modern, were based on the values referred to in the previous section.
They will also find that when these values move from one civilization to
another, they undergo a process of development and refinement. This
represents the contribution of the ancient civilizations to humanity
at the same time as showing the developments made by more recent civilizations to the values they received from their ancestors, elevating them
to a higher plane and opening new vistas before them. This does not
negate the fact that the contribution of some civilizations to this refining
process has been greater than others. For example, the largest contribution by far to developing the contemporary values of work has been
made by Western civilization which, as the birthplace of the Industrial
Revolution, provided a favourable climate for the refinement and conse-
cration of these values. Nevertheless, the values of progress in general
and the values of work (including modern management concepts) in particular have been developed over the ages by humanity at large and not
by any specific civilization, even if the ability of the West to put them to
optimal use makes them appear to be products of Western civilization.

The 'humanistic' nature of these values is borne out by the fact that
in the course of only one century – the twentieth – they passed over
from an environment that was purely Western to others which followed altogether different models of civilization, such as Japan and
tens of countries in Asia and Latin America, which adopted these values as part of their culture complex, and put them to use in fuelling the
engine of their remarkable economic growth. This proves that even if
at one stage they took root and flourished in a Western environment,
they are, in the final analysis, human, not Western values.

2. OBSTACLES ON THE ROAD TO PROGRESS

A. Mistaking Ideas for the Remedy

A characteristic shared by many of the countries which face break-
downs in the machinery of public life, and which are now seeking the

road to a better future, is the conviction that their hopes could be ful-
filled and their goals achieved if only they had 'good' ideas. But it is a
dangerous fallacy to think that ideas might be a panacea for all ills. It is
not ideas alone that can improve reality or create a better future.
Herein lies the difference between intellectuals and philosophers, most
of whom are incapable of managing a small business or reforming even
a tiny village, and top management and business leaders who have the
necessary skills to transform reality through actions, not words.

Moreover, the search for good ideas is both a lengthy process and
one that creates a divisive and polemical climate, as the proponents of
any given idea debate ideological differences. What is really needed is
people who epitomize the ideas which can serve as a bridge towards a
better future. It should be remembered that great civilizations were
built less on abstract ideas than by actions – drive, spirit and imagination, yes, but essentially by individuals with the will and skill to turn
dreams into reality. And if it is axiomatic that a man and his ideas constitute an integral whole, it follows that the ideas needed to reform the
present and pave the way to a better future will not come from people
whose ideas are based less on principles than on expediency.

B. The Societal Structure

One of the biggest blunders committed by tens of Third World countries is to have turned the social pyramid upside down, thereby creating
a new pyramid which allows the least qualified members of society to
occupy the top positions. Meanwhile, in developed countries, the societal pyramid is constructed so that only the best, in terms of ability,
intelligence, culture, ethics and motivation, can rise to the top. These
elites command the decision-making process, guiding their countries
along what they claim to be the best course. Third World countries,
where because of historical conditions state power is usually seized
through coups, are subject to a different system based on personal
loyalty and trust, in which people are chosen for their allegiance to the
ruler rather than on merit. As a result, the top 5 per cent of positions
are not occupied by society's best but by elements which disseminate
the most inferior and abject of values throughout society as a whole.

In developed societies, social Darwinism (the law of natural selection) prevails, based on the selection by society of its best citizens for
the highest posts, and this is a dynamic process. In the often regressive
societies of the Third World, social Darwinism is not allowed to operate.
Rather, public life is based on loyalty and allegiance, cronyism and, at
a later stage, corruption. While corruption is part and parcel of the

human condition, it only proliferates in an atmosphere of inferior values where incompetent bureaucrats hold the top positions; in countries where the societal pyramid is based on the principles of social Darwinism, it can be checked and ferreted out before harming the infrastructure.

C. The Wrong Human Calibre

Public life should be administered by people who have actually succeeded in the context of these objectives, not by functionaries whose ideas, brains and objectives have been atrophied through long years of state hegemony over economic life.

The mechanism which can achieve the desired change lies in using talents similar to those which led the NIC countries of Asia from underdevelopment to remarkable economic vigour and success. The importance of this mechanism cannot be overrated: once it is set in motion, it is only a matter of time before the desired reforms effect eventual transformation.

To bring about change from the bottom up is virtually impossible in the current set-up. Perhaps the main factor working against it is the time needed for the values of change to flow from the base of society to its summit. This could take decades, even centuries. The change that could be achieved in a generation is dependent on competent individuals who are ready to act in accordance with the new values and criteria and apply the successful experiment of the NIC of Asia.

D. Blinding Illusion

There is no doubt that the historical and cultural conditions in which Arab civilization evolved have affected the way Arabs think. One of the most important specifics of Arab thinking is a tendency to confuse the possible with the impossible, a certain romanticism which often blurs the fine distinctions between what should be, what could be and what will be. Because of this tendency, the Arabs have allowed many historical opportunities to slip through their fingers; rejecting offers that they often later realized would have been to their advantage. It is thus vital that those who mould the options, whether in foreign or domestic policy, should be able to distinguish between reality and wishful thinking.

As I said earlier, socialism has fallen apart, taking with it its failed experience and ideology. Mourning it, and struggling to make its traces and marks survive, is a futile exercise which can only drag societies even further backwards. Instead of living in the memory of a past which proved disastrous, people should learn to pick the fruits of political, social and economic experiences which have led to the prosperity and success of other societies which have progressed far from ideology.

In other words, those who are still attached to a history which reminds them of their own better days should come to face the fact that the welfare of society as a whole lies in their detaching themselves from their nostalgia, hence from the principles and value systems which, as I said, have no place in today's reality, and using their competences and abilities to drive their society on the road of the civilized human march, along with those who have progressed in other parts of the world.

Two main features characterize the world of today and promise that the world is and will become ever more 'internationalist' in nature, as old frontiers break down and markets and communities open to all. Thanks to recent developments on the political front, as well as to the information revolution, the world has been transformed into a global village displaying very different characteristics from any we have known in the past.

In this new world of accelerated change and greater interdependence, decision-makers will have to involve themselves intimately with the specifics of economic and social life in their countries – that is, they will have to focus on the trees rather than maintain an overall view of the forest, as they have done in the past.

These two features will lead to the emergence of a new breed of politicians. The challenges posed by an open world in which trade competition will become ever more intense, call for leaders who are in effect executive managers, not politicians in the traditional sense of the word. A politician will need more than judiciousness and level-headedness in the new set-up. To be successful and effective, he/she will need to have a broad grasp of many areas of public life, paralleling the managerial talents of top chief executive officers.

Singapore's prime minister[1] who, in just under thirty years, transformed his country from a stereotypically poor and underdeveloped Southeast Asian state into an outstanding success story, should serve as an example for leaders hoping to give their countries an edge in a fiercely competitive world.

E. The Conspiracy Theory

There is a pervasive belief among many Third World peoples that certain forces, including some Western intelligence agencies, are involved in a conspiracy aimed at achieving global domination and grinding the poor countries underfoot. The conspiracy theory is often tinged with an ideological hue, either by diehard socialists or by others obsessed with the idea that they are the main targets of a conspiracy, which of course exists only in their minds.

Another mechanism which fuels the belief in the conspiracy theory among millions of people is the Western economic system, which is based on competition, both inside and outside the advanced capitalist societies. If one aspect of competition is that various economic units vie for a bigger share of the market by enhancing their products and services, expanding operations and maximizing profits, the other is that a bigger share for some means a smaller share for others. The spirit of competition is the cornerstone of Western liberal democracy, and it is normal that it should govern the relations between the economic units, governments and companies of the outside world. In other words, if it is logical that those who compete among themselves should also compete with others, then the same logic dictates that they should seek to maintain their edge as seller to the others' buyers, producers to their consumers, and exporters to their importers.

Thus, when the proponents of the conspiracy theory accuse the West of wanting Third World countries to remain at their present level of development, they are at the same time quite right and completely wrong. They are right because the laws of the market impose their own logic, and within that logic the West would not like its domination of world markets challenged. They are wrong because there is no conspiracy, only the natural workings of the machinery of the capitalist economic (and hence political) system. Arabs should seek to understand the inner workings of the system and use them to their advantage, if they hope to have a place in a world governed by the law of survival of the fittest. They should also remember that the activities of institutions, including the government, in countries with a market economy, happen in accordance with corporate law mechanisms.

F. The Identity and Specificity Crisis

If the Arabs' hopes of bringing about the fateful transformation that can lead them towards a brighter future are ever to materialize, they must overcome the identity crisis that has held them in its grip for so many years. It is high time that the Egyptians (being a good example of Arabic-speaking societies) should come to terms with the fact that they are, before all else, Egyptians. That is not to say their identity does not include an Arab component, only that it is not the primary component. For instance, their literature is essentially Arab, including works by Christian Arabs, but that is not enough to stamp them with an all-Arab identity. As to Islam, while there is no doubt that it is one of the most basic elements in Egypt's civilizational make-up, clearly Egyptians, Nigerians, Pakistanis and Malaysians are not one and the same thing.

In societies where people are aware of the background of wealth, fame and success, and where this background is based on hard work, struggle and ability, then and only then will people and society accept wealth, fame and success as the natural result of visible processes. More often than not, success stories of this kind are the object of admiration and respect.

When people realize how much effort and will went into achieving success, whether in building up a huge fortune or attaining a high position, they will accept it. But when personal relations, abuse of power, opportunism, corruption and darkness are the main elements behind many examples of fortune and fame, two phenomena are bound to emerge:

1. The first is the lack of respect with which people come to regard examples of fortune and fame, and the widespread feeling that these are the fruits of dishonourable and manipulative practices conducted outside the channels of accountability.
2. The second is a refusal to admit the right of the rich and famous to enjoy their 'ill-gotten' gains, claiming their success was attained more by chance and opportunity than by hard work or exceptional abilities. This naturally creates an atmosphere of envy and frustration.

By allowing mediocre people to rise to the pinnacles of wealth and success, the system itself breeds envy and hatred in society, devalues the virtues of excellence and hard work, and encourages young people to seek short cuts to success. After all, why should they strive for excellence in a society where success stories based on true talent and ability are few, while those based on chance, nepotism and the exchange of favours abound?

NOTE

1. Lee Kuan Yew; prime minister of Singapore from 1959 to 1990.

6

The Heart and Mind of the Middle East

Talking about each and every society in the Arab countries would require volumes that would exceed the intended size of this book. Since the aspects of Egyptian life bear a close resemblance to those of most of the Arabic-speaking societies, Egypt will constantly be referred to as an example which applies to the majority of these societies.

1. THE EGYPTIAN IDENTITY

Throughout most of its modern history, which began with Mohamed 'Ali's accession to power in 1805,[1] Egypt has suffered from a kind of split personality. To my mind, this stems from the educational and cultural poverty that has marked Egyptians' lives over the last two centuries. This has left some of them unable to come to terms with the challenges of the present and preferring to seek refuge in the past, while others turn to the Western model of civilization, adopting its cultural mores and lifestyles. It seems that the most difficult option is the one many of them have abandoned, which is simply to be themselves, here and now. This entails sifting through their cultural heritage and discarding those elements which were merely the product of a specific time and circumstances, as well as adopting from the Western model elements that are the fruits of the collective human experience. The most important of these are not, contrary to conventional wisdom, science and technology, but the values of progress, creativity, work and innovation.

The lack of a common framework of identity has led to acute tensions between past, present and future. For some, the only acceptable framework is the past, whether the distant past as in the case of the fundamentalists, or the recent past as in the case of the Nasserites.[2] Others reject the past in favour of a future whose features and identity are still far from clear. An initiative should be launched to bring about a reconciliation between past, present and future, based on the general consensus that Egypt deserves a future better than its present or its past.

Although Mohamed 'Ali was a great man, his example was partially negated by some of what happened during or after his reign. The same applies to Sa'd Zaghloul,[3] Gamal Abdel-Nasser,[4] Anwar Sadat[5] and the other leaders of Egypt's national struggle for independence. Now, however, fundamental reforms that properly address the present need to be imposed, if there is to be a better future for the sons and daughters of this nation.

The dichotomy that exists in the Egyptian psyche is not new. Reading the now-declassified dispatches sent home by Britain's representatives in Egypt between 1882 and 1952,[6] I was struck – and pained – by how often they reported on 'deep divisions among the Egyptians'. It was particularly galling to read Sir Evelyn Baring's[7] account of his farewell party. Sir Evelyn, the earl of Cromer, was the British consul-general and de facto governor of Egypt. His farewell party was attended by Egypt's political leaders, each of whom took him aside to complain of the others and seek his support against them.

The deep divisions among Egyptians are symptomatic of an inability on the part of many to distinguish between past, present and future. But for this confusion, there would have been basic level of agreement between them. However, because of a severe decline in education and culture, exacerbated by a sequence of leaders who, for over a century following 'Ali's abdication, were not the most intelligent, cultured or honest individuals, nor necessarily among the most able and talented, this trait became so imbued that it seemed to be part of the Egyptians' genetic make-up.

2. A STRONG INTERIOR IS IMPERATIVE

Most political thinkers have a list of priorities that they feel committed to writing about; in my case, the key priority is definitely that of building a strong Egyptian interior: a healthy society with a substantial middle class, a stable economy, progressive education, and a cultural environment that keeps abreast of the times; a society that, moreover, maintains a thorough knowledge of, and pride in, its history and heritage – though without falling into the trap of worshipping the past. To those with other priorities heading their lists, I would say that none of them can be achieved without first establishing a strong, stable, prosperous interior. There are those who dream of a successful pan-Arab national project, but this can never be realized without first establishing a robust Egyptian interior; others dream of an Egypt playing a prominent regional or even international role, but again I repeat: this can never happen until Egypt is strong, stable and prosperous from within. This is a prerequisite for the fulfilment of any of the Egyptians' other aims or aspirations.

In spite of my admiration for Mohamed 'Ali, whom most scholars, researchers and writers commonly refer to as 'the founder of modern Egypt', it is an undeniable fact that his involvement with external issues distracted him from his primary mission of building an Egypt that was strong internally, with disastrous results that had far-reaching repercussions. If Mohamed 'Ali had only concentrated his efforts on strengthening the country from within, Egypt would have been well equipped to play the pivotal role that is its due by virtue of its geographical, historic and cultural distinctiveness. Conversely, this insistence on focusing on issues other than building a strong interior systematically erodes any efforts made internally – a state of affairs which has been consistently repeated throughout the history of modern Egypt.

One of Egypt's biggest problems is that numerous factors entice it to get involved in matters outside its borders. The problem does not lie in its involvement per se, but rather in the fact that Egypt takes this role upon itself without first completing its primary, sacred objective of building a strong, stable and prosperous interior. This haste ultimately and inevitably leads to two disastrous outcomes: the failure of most of its external missions, and a serious delay in the internal building process. To be fair, the decision-making process under presidents Sadat and Mubarak[8] has been characterized by a high degree of pragmatism in the field of foreign policy. On the domestic front, however, things are different. Although decisions here too are informed in large measure by practical considerations, many of Egypt's public personalities still tend to confuse reality with hopes. It is important to understand that for domestic issues, people of a different calibre are needed than for foreign policy matters. At the same time, internal options are closely linked to ideologies. This leaves the field open to beliefs, views and solutions stemming from a past which, though totally discredited, still has representatives in key posts. It should be obvious to any observer of the Egyptian scene that men and ideas of the past are obstructing those of the present and future. It should also be obvious that their motives are not purely ideological, but linked to personal interests and careerism.

It is my unswerving conviction that the most important task facing Egyptians today is to concentrate all their efforts upon achieving a strong, progressive, prosperous and stable interior that is, moreover, in perfect harmony with its past and its present. This can only be achieved with an all-out campaign in which they all join forces to instil and disseminate the values of progress amongst all those occupying key positions, and hence serving as role models, and simultaneously establishing an effective educational system, the prime mission of which would be to infuse the minds of the sons and daughters of Egypt with these values. I must add that this task will be impossible to achieve unless a radical change in the religious communications being disseminated (whether Muslim or Christian) is brought about, for it is an undeniable fact that religious teachings, together with the media, remain the most important factors influencing public opinion in Egypt.

There are those who dream of Egypt as it was before 1952; some pine for Nasser's Egypt, others for the days of Sadat. A thinker who can keep his/her emotions in check, and judge impartially and rationally, would choose the quality of the middle class that existed in the pre-1952 days, but not the scarcity of its numbers – or the masses of people who lived below the poverty line in pitiful conditions that are a disgrace to all Egyptians. From the Egypt of the 1950s and 1960s, he/she would choose its dream of an extensive middle class resting upon a solid economic and cultural base; and from the Sadat era, the supremacy of dialogue and rational thinking in some cases.

I write this with the firm belief that wasting time in recriminations, and in censuring and condemning others, is an exercise in futility. Rather, a state of reconciliation should be negotiated between those of different views, bearing in mind that this can only be achieved by launching a comprehensive initiative to instil and disseminate the values of progress. Let us view the different stages of Egypt's history with objectivity and without exaggerating the advantages and disadvantages of each phase – again, this will not be possible except in a cultural and educational environment in which the values of progress have been implanted.

The biggest challenge facing Egypt today concerns the middle class, who have been – and are still being – subjected to a bewildering plethora of economic, educational and cultural dynamics that have led to the point where one is hard put to define what exactly constitutes the middle class in Egypt today. Real progress in any society is not contingent upon the existence of an upper class of high calibre, but depends, rather, upon the quality, size and calibre of its middle class, which again is inextricably linked to the extent to which the values of progress are implanted in this vital sector of society.

To sum up, Egypt's problems cannot be solved without first creating an environment imbued with the values of progress. Then, and only then, will Egypt's role beyond its borders become a reality, and indeed an incontestable right; for Egypt is historically, geographically and culturally the only Middle Eastern country equipped to assume the role of leader in the region – but only after first establishing a strong and progressive interior.

3. ARE EGYPTIANS READY FOR PROGRESS?

Two properties falsely and unfairly attributed to Egypt and the Egyptians by ordinary people and by experts, by foreigners and by the Egyptians themselves, have been repeated so often that they have come to be regarded as incontrovertible truths. The first is that the country and its people are capable of producing only one form of government: a highly centralized political organization dominated by an oligarchy wielding absolute power. The common belief is that throughout its long history, Egypt managed to transform all alternative forms of government into this uniquely Egyptian formula, in which centralization attained its most extreme form. The second property that conventional wisdom attributes to Egyptians is that they are not ready for democracy, on the grounds that the level of education and culture of a high percentage among them is below the minimum required for such a proactive form of political participation.

The first allegation is easily refuted. For a start, very little is known about the political life and form of government that prevailed in Ancient Egypt, a period stretching from approximately 3000 BC to 300 BC. We are not in possession of any scientific data on how the mechanisms of government functioned for close on three thousand years. Even if folk legends about the extreme centralization of Pharaonic rule are true, the practices of that far-off time cannot be extrapolated onto the present. Moving on to a less remote, better-documented past, we find that from 300 BC until the middle of the twentieth century, the Egyptians were ruled by foreigners. If they were kept in check by means of an extremely centralized form of government, it was neither by their choice, nor of their making. In other words, it was a formula imposed on them by their foreign rulers. The years following the end of the British protectorate saw Egypt's experiment with representative government, the antithesis of centralization. While it is difficult to claim that during the heyday of modern parliamentary life – which flourished from 1924 to 1952 – true democracy prevailed, it is also difficult to deny the existence of a dynamic Egyptian nationalist movement which waged a tireless struggle against centralization. The majority party at the time, the Wafd, participated actively in the struggle, as did the minority parties. A striking example of the unified front presented by all the opposition parties in this connection is the stand adopted by the Liberal Constitutionalist Party towards the attempts made by King Fouad and Ismail Sidqi Pasha in the first three years of the 1930s, to strengthen the powers of the monarch and curtail those of parliament.[9] If Egypt's experiment with liberalism was marred by many mistakes, its greatest achievement was the promotion and development of a vibrant national movement which fought valiantly to end a system of rule based on the absolute centralization of power. Despite a number of setbacks, its efforts were beginning to bear fruit. After 1952, however, the drive towards decentralization was replaced by a drive towards even greater centralization, as the new order sought to tighten its political control over the country. This is best illustrated by what happened to the institutions of the *omda* and *sheikh el balad* (the village headman and his deputy). Traditionally performing the function of local governments or local security agencies in Egypt's villages, they used to go about their business without referring to the central government. Left pretty much to their own devices, they used to stand as a symbol of the decentralized exercise of power. When this system was abolished and replaced by a system in which the occupants of these posts were appointed by the central government, this brought one of the most prominent aspects of Egyptian decentralization to an end.

Thus, the allegation that throughout their history Egyptians produced only a highly centralized form of government is groundless. For twenty-two centuries, centralization – assuming it existed – was imposed on them by foreign rulers. Throughout the years of Egypt's early experiment with democracy (1924–52), the Egyptian national movement fought for a more decentralized form of government. After 1952, greater centralization was the natural objective of a regime that did not hide its allegiance to the one-party system.

There is no doubt that, historically, Egypt has produced excessive centralization at the superstructural level – that is, at the pinnacle of power. But this did not apply to all levels; otherwise, we would not have known the form of local government that existed when the *omda* and the *sheikh el balad* performed the function they did for decades before they became government-appointed employees.

As to the second allegation, which is that Egyptians are not ready for democracy because of their low level of education and culture, this can be even more easily refuted. History proves that democracy took root in England at the beginning of the nineteenth century, when illiteracy rates were extremely high. And despite the fact that the ordinary American citizen receives a higher level of education than his Egyptian counterpart, he/she is often incapable of making a considered choice between various options, not to mention the fact that his/her knowledge of the outside world is practically non-existent. Democracy in all its contemporary forms is based on the choices made by the elected representatives of the people who conduct political life on their behalf. Thus, democracy in and of itself is not above reproach; as much as it can be an engine for good, it can also lead to disastrous mistakes. A flagrant example of democracy gone awry is the case of Adolph Hitler, who was elected to power in Germany by due democratic process.[10] Thus, the essence of democracy is not the high level of education of the people, but the mechanisms of change and rotation of power. This means that democracy does not represent the acme of perfection, for there is no absolute perfection in any human endeavour. Rather, it is a better system than others. Its relative superiority derives from the fact that it does not lead to the emergence of the biggest defect in human nature, which is the continued presence of people in power without a time limit. The availability of a mechanism for the rotation of power acts as a check on the human defect that allows people to believe they can remain in power for as long as they live.

It is clear from all the above that those who claim that Egyptians are congenitally disposed to a centralized form of government, and that they are not ready for democracy, are way off the mark. These false allegations serve only those who would deprive the Egyptians of the finest achievement of humankind: democracy, which brought about a fundamental transformation in the concept of governance in the interests of the citizen.

4. OBSTACLES ON EGYPT'S ROAD TO PROGRESS

A. Management of Resources (Including Egypt's Public Sector)

To the same extent that it inspired a great surge of national pride and joy, the Nobel Prize for Chemistry awarded to Ahmed Zeweil[11] raised many questions about the state of scientific research and technological progress in Egypt. Although much has been said on the subject, I had the opportunity to hear two points of view on the same day; I believe that these encapsulate all that can possibly be said in this connection.

With all due respect to the proponents of the two viewpoints expressed on the day in question, I believe that one was completely off the mark, and the other absolutely correct. According to the first view, the only thing preventing Egypt from being among the advanced nations of the world in the field of scientific research and its technological applications is a lack of resources. The other view holds that the problem lies in the climate of scientific research, which lacks the spirit of teamwork and the institutional framework which can serve and support the role of the researcher.

From my long experience in the world of management, I believe that the people who rely on the 'lack-of-resources' argument are motivated by an understandable – if misplaced – belief that this excuse absolves them of responsibility for the present state of affairs in the fields of theoretical and applied sciences.

There are tens of countries with a lower per capita income than Egypt's and with huge economic problems that have surpassed Egypt's in these fields, but I will cite just one example here, namely India, whose performance in these fields, particularly in the areas of atomic research and computer technology, is impressive by any standards. Thanks to its scientific and technological achievements, India is now a nuclear power. It is also the third largest exporter of software programmes in the world and is expected to move up shortly to second place, right behind the United States.

The massive economic and social problems plaguing India, including a severe shortage of financial resources, have not prevented it from scoring remarkable results in these areas (atomic research and computer technology), which are both based on advanced scientific research. While there are many other similar examples, this example alone is sufficient to rebut the argument that what prevents Egyptians from building an advanced and efficient scientific infrastructure is nothing but a lack of resources.

To attribute the Egyptians' inability to develop an advanced scientific infrastructure to a lack of resources is wrong, not only because it is based on faulty reasoning, but also because it allows Egyptians to indulge in a rationale of justification that prevents them from exercising the required degree of self-criticism. What Egypt really lacks is modern working methods in the field of scientific research, governed by up-to-date management systems that can provide the necessary elements of success by nurturing people of superior ability, developing the spirit of teamwork, putting an end to the practice of repressing talented people, and removing from the world of scientific research the values of careerism and political ambition that have pervaded it over the last few decades.

The problem is thus one of management rather than of resources. Overcoming it entails removing from the management process the elements that have led to Egypt's present state of backwardness in the domain of scientific research. Egyptians must have the courage to admit that unless they diagnose the ills and change the general climate prevailing in that domain, they will never be able to overcome the present state of affairs. It is necessary here to entrust Egyptian scientists living abroad with the task of diagnosing the ills and prescribing the means of treating them, as the members of the local scientific community are often too close to the trees to see the forest. Moreover, they could find it embarrassing to direct any criticism at their administrative superiors. That is not to say that Egyptian scientists are unable to diagnose the problem, define its reasons and propose the mode of treatment, only that what might be embarrassing for them would be less so for Egyptian scientists living abroad. Such hierarchical constraints can be a real obstacle on the way to reforming the scientific climate in Egypt.

Another obstacle on Egypt's road to progress is the Egyptians' attitude towards what is generally agreed to be a severe management problem. The problem, which I believe is the reason for the failure of the public sector, the erratic performance of the private sector and the poor performance of government departments and service sectors, is openly acknowledged, but no practical steps are being taken to overcome it. Instead, a great deal of energy is expended in assigning blame. Some attribute the acute shortage of management talents to the fact that the educational system is incapable of producing citizens who can become effective managers. Others blame the system of work, particularly the systems of promotion and the selection of leaders on the basis of seniority, and the absence of programmes for the formation of effective managers. Others, still, see the problem as resulting from the precedence given in the work environment to subjective considerations over objective criteria. Finally, there are those who say that the problem arises from the fact that Egyptians are out of touch with modern management systems and techniques in advanced societies. Thus everyone acknowledges the existence of the disease, many are willing to offer a diagnostic opinion as to its cause, but there is no attempt to prescribe the medicine by which it can be cured. This is yet another example of the contradictory approach to the problems besetting society, an approach that is caught between action and inaction. Action in the direction of coming to grips with the problem is represented in the willingness to admit that it exists; inaction is represented in an inability – not to say unwillingness

– to remove the causes that created the problem in the first place. Where radical surgery is required to excise the root causes of the disease, Egyptians choose instead to alleviate its symptoms by means of palliatives that can, at best, offer only temporary relief.

B. Stagnant Thinking

The idea for this section took shape while I was watching a panel discussion between two distinguished Egyptian intellectuals over the agreement reached in Nairobi (some time ago) between the Sudan People's Liberation Army (SPLA), led by the late John Garang,[12] and the Khartoum government. The debate was a study in contrasts, an exchange between two men belonging to different stages of historical development. One came across as a throwback to a bygone era, his cultural terms of reference and political discourse locked in the mindset which held sway in the region up to the 1960s, while the other, despite being an octogenarian, spoke the language of the age and displayed a sound grasp of the profound changes which have swept the world over the last thirty years. Going beyond the static confines of the question put to him by his interlocutor, who asked him whether the Nairobi agreement was 'good or bad' for Egypt, the latter launched into an elaborate reply which can be summarized as follows:

> The answer depends on us. If we continue to look upon Sudan as an Egyptian invention ... if we continue to talk about Sudan as though it were a part of Egypt like it was in the days of Mohamed 'Ali and his sons ... if we continue to warn that any encroachment on the sources of the Nile waters will be met with dire consequences ... that kind of static, backward-looking thinking will inevitably lead to a situation in which the agreement will be harmful for us. On the other hand, if we place matters in their proper perspective and deal with the issue in accordance with the realities of the age ... if we can establish a healthy and constructive dialogue based on mutual respect with all the concerned parties ... if we work to forge common interests with those parties in the context of the new realities and not on the basis of antiquated slogans, then the Nairobi agreement can be beneficial for Egypt.

Apparently not realizing that his question had been answered, the first panellist continued to press his interlocutor for a reply. As I looked on in consternation, it occurred to me that what we were seeing was more than a simple misunderstanding: that it was in fact indicative of a much deeper problem, a kind of intellectual inertia that has come to characterize the thought processes of many among us, public figures and private individuals alike. The problem manifests itself in a tendency to indulge in what I call static thinking, where the terms of reference are not present-day realities but clichés and slogans which, though obsolete, continue to be regarded by many as the ultimate truth, as constants carved in stone. Actually, the word 'constants' is meaningless in the rapidly changing landscape of today's world, even when used in reference to what makes up the Egyptian and Arab cultural specificity. For what is specific to the Egyptian or Arab culture – or to any culture for that matter – includes not only positive but also negative features, all of which are amenable to change. In other words, they are variables, not constants. But instead of placing their faith in the only real constants in our world, which are science, strategic interests and humanity, Egyptians and Arabs choose to wallow in nostalgia, clinging to pan-nationalism and narrow parochialism as though they were immutable truths.

The greatest proof that Egyptian thinking is inward-looking, past-oriented and out of step with the times lies in the fact that the outside world finds Egypt's slogans totally incomprehensible and is consequently not interested in reading what its writers and intellectuals have to say. Of course, this does not apply to the works of the creative writers, who do have an audience transcending the language barrier; nor does it apply to the few political writers, whose works have an appreciative audience in the outside world, not because their readers necessarily agree with what they say, but because of the high quality of their writing. By and large, however, Egypt has dug a cave for itself, cut off from the rest of humanity thanks to a static mindset that ignores the realities of our time and the new balances of power. It has managed to isolate itself even from such staunch former allies as India, China, the countries of Eastern Europe, and Russia, which have distanced themselves from Egypt's position on many issues. The reason is that these countries have evolved with the times and adapted themselves to the requirements of the age, while Egypt remains locked in a fantasy world of its own making, speaking a language that is incomprehensible to all but the initiated – a world in which anachronistic slogans are still widely regarded as sacrosanct, immutable constants. This has resulted not only in the Egyptians' growing isolation from the outside world and in alienating their former allies, but also in a disastrous internal situation marked by a pattern of lost opportunities and a climate inimical to democracy and development.

This may seem at first glance to be an abstract, theoretical approach to the problems plaguing Egypt, but in fact it is quite the opposite. How can Egyptians hope to make any headway in the area of educational reform, for example, when the calls for reform – and there are many – come up against stiff resistance to the need for fundamental changes in their educational philosophy and curricula and an insistence on maintaining the status quo? How can there be political reform when there is an adamant refusal even to consider changing any of the pillars on which their political life rests? How can there be economic reform without introducing radical changes to those aspects of Egypt's economic life that render the investment climate in this country incompatible with the requirements of international economic life? In short, Egypt is trying to square the circle, at the same time claiming that it aspires to improve its lot while clinging to its old ways. To expect its situation to change for the better while refusing to change many of the features of its political, economic and educational landscape is a contradiction in terms, and the sooner the Egyptians realize this, the closer they will be to achieving the progress to which they aspire.

I have no doubt that the culture of stagnation, or opposition to change, in which Egypt, as an example of the Arabic-speaking societies, seems to be mired stems either from a fear of the unknown, a reluctance to abandon the safety of a present with which Egyptians are familiar – however dismal it may be – for a future whose features remain obscure, or from the ferocious resistance of certain elements with vested interests in the present set-up to any change which could threaten those interests. Nevertheless, from the perspective of modern management science, I am willing to accept the argument that while change is inevitable, it must be gradual to ensure social peace. I may differ with the argument as to the required rate of change, but I cannot deny its validity, provided it is not used to justify inaction, as this will only exacerbate the festering stagnation which has become a feature of the Egyptians' reality and render the problems they are facing even more intractable than they already are.

To clarify the picture further, it might be useful to cite some examples here. The first is that economic statistics confirm that an annual economic growth rate of between 8 per cent and 10 per cent must be sustained for a full decade if the economic prosperity necessary for social peace is to be achieved. I would add here that economic prosperity alone, without modern education and public participation in political life, cannot guarantee social and political peace. Another economic fact of life is that sustained economic growth at the rate of 8 per cent to 10 per cent annually is impossible if we rely exclusively on Egypt's own resources (the state and the savings of citizens).

The inescapable conclusion to be drawn from the above is that if Egypt wants to attain the required rate of growth, it must attract foreign investments – either direct or indirect – in a systematic manner. This leads us to the following question: Given that Egypt realises that foreign investments are indispensable for economic growth, why are investments not pouring in at the required rate? The answer is simply that Egypt's declared aim of attracting foreign investments is not accompanied by a will to change a whole array of disincentives that effectively keep such investments away. Once again it is caught red-handed in a flagrant contradiction by setting a goal for itself while doing nothing to make it achievable. Had it not been for the culture of rigid adherence to the status quo that dominates its life, Egypt would have admitted that foreign investments are not coming its way at the desired rate because investors are put off by a long list of obstacles, and then concrete measures would have been taken to remove those obstacles. But to allege that foreign investments are not flowing in because there is a conspiracy against Egypt or because foreign investors are not aware of the attractive investment climate that it is offering them, is to act like a patient who knows that he is ill but insists that he will recover without taking the prescribed medication.

C. The English Language – a Sample of Education

The discussions I had in more than ten universities with hundreds of faculty members, undergraduates and postgraduate students, many from Third World countries such as India and China, confirmed the validity of my views on the subject of education in Egypt.

Although there is no lack of examples of the regression of the level of education, I will cite just one, namely the inability of the Arabic-speaking societies, including the Egyptians, to act in the light of two facts that are known to all. The first is that knowledge of the English language, spoken and written, is one of the most important requirements of our age, and that it is impossible to keep up with modern science, culture and knowledge without a sound command of the English language. Recognition of this fact brought about important changes in societies such as France, Germany and Japan which, until the 1970s, resisted the widespread use of English out of a misplaced sense of national pride. Today, the situation is just the opposite because the requirements of the age imposed themselves on those societies.

The second fact is that Egyptian government schools in the 1920s and 1930s produced graduates with a sound command of English, and sometimes of French as well, in addition to Arabic. Although Egyptians are all well aware of these facts, and although they all tirelessly repeat the need for educational reform, the new generations graduating from other than foreign schools have no knowledge of English, while the graduates of foreign schools have poor knowledge of Arabic. Here, again, Egyptians are caught in a flagrant contradiction between a consensus on the goal – in this case educational reform – and complete failure when it comes to tackling an aspect of the required reform that is well within their means to correct. This particular aspect can be addressed in isolation from the many other shortcomings in their educational system, and can go far towards bringing about the reform to which they all aspire. I am talking about the low English-language proficiency of the teachers entrusted with producing future generations with a sound command of a language that has become an international lingua franca.

A recent conversation I had with one of Egypt's most successful governors brought home the horror of the situation. Apparently the results of a survey he commissioned his aides to conduct, on the academic qualifications of the English-language teachers in his governorate, showed that 80 per cent of them had never received a formal education in English but had specialized in other areas, such as history, sociology or geography. Stunned by the findings, the governor has embarked on reforming the school system in his bailiwick, but it remains to be seen whether his well-intentioned endeavour to bring about the required changes can succeed in a cultural context that is so resistant to change. It was not difficult to discover the disturbing facts revealed by the survey he commissioned; the difficulty lies in standing up to the well-entrenched defenders of the status quo.

Until the Egyptians recognize the importance of making the values of progress part and parcel of the educational process, their students will continue to lag far behind their peers in the advanced countries of the world, not in terms of intelligence but of acquired skills. In the case of developed societies, these skills evolve as a natural by-product of an educational system based on the set of values mentioned earlier, while Egyptian students are locked behind high walls throughout their school and university years, prisoners of a system based on stuffing their minds with massive amounts of often useless information, and on making them learn by rote.

If the stark picture I have painted of some of the problems Egypt is facing is painful to contemplate, my excuse is that I find what Gibran

Khalil Gibran said, in his book *The Storms* (published in 1920), as relevant today as it was when he wrote it more than eighty years ago, that many physicians in the East attend to the sick, but they do not treat them with other than temporary palliatives that extend the duration of their malady, but do not cure it.

NOTES

1. (c. 1769–1849). Governor of Egypt; founder of modern Egypt and of the dynasty which ruled Egypt until the expulsion of King Farouk on July 26, 1952 (followed by the abolishment of the monarchy on 18 June 1953).
2. The Nasserites are the followers and adherents of the political ideology known as Nasserism. This was the term applied to the political philosophy of former Egyptian President Nasser (see Chapter 2, note 20). It included international neutralism, Arab nationalism and socialism. Following Sadat's reforms (see Chapter 4, note 9) Nasserism came to represent the views of those opposed to his policy, i.e. political but mainly economic capitalist liberalization. On 19 April 1992, the Nasserite Arab Democratic Party was formally approved and given permission to participate in Egyptian elections.
3. (1859–1927). Egyptian political figure; served as prime minister of Egypt from 26 January 1924 to 24 November 1924.
4. See Chapter 2, note 20.
5. See Chapter 4, note 9.
6. Period during which Britain had interests in Egypt. 1882 marks the beginning of the British occupation; 1952 is the year of the revolution that ousted the king and foreign interests from Egypt.
7. (1841–1917). First earl of Cromer; British diplomat and colonial administrator; British controller-general in Egypt (1879), then agent and consul-general in Egypt (1883–1907).
8. (Born 1928). Fourth president of Egypt (since 1981); successor of President Anwar Sadat (see Chapter 4, note 9).
9. The most significant of these attempts was the abolishment of the 1923 Constitution in 1930 and the issuing of a new constitution (the 1930 Constitution) that shifted a great deal of the authority from the hands of the representatives of the Egyptian people (in the parliament) to the king and his executive power.
10. See Chapter 2, note 17.
11. See Chapter 6, note 11.
12. (1945–2005). Sudanese leader of the Sudan People's Liberation Army and vice-president of Sudan (2005); killed in a helicopter crash.

7

Eliminating Obstacles

I must confess that I have dozens of habits – all one way or another related to reading – that I can only justify as being driven by nostalgia. One of these habits is to return again and yet again to four of the works I prefer, namely: Ahmed Shawki's[1] poem about Ahmed Loutfy El Sayed[2] on the occasion of the latter's translation of one of Aristotle's books; Ahmed Loutfy El Sayed's translated version of that book: *Politics by Aristotle*; the third part of *The Wednesday Talk* by Taha Hussein,[3] which contains an article discussing the mentioned three works (Shawki's poem, Aristotle's book, and Ahmed Loutfy El Sayed's); and finally, *The Story Of My Life* by Ahmed Loutfy El Sayed, published in 1962 on the occasion of the venerable professor's ninetieth birthday (he was born on 15 January 1872).

My motives for returning to these readings are twofold, and are, as I said, both related to nostalgia. The first is my infatuation with the works of Aristotle, Ahmed Loutfy El Sayed and Taha Hussein; the second is my fascination with that specific period in history (the 1920s), when Egypt's leading intellectuals avidly pursued their dream of modernization and enlightenment, with a keenness equalled only by their passion for the Renaissance and for the civilization of ancient Greece. Whenever Ahmed Loutfy El Sayed translated some of the writings of Aristotle, Taha Hussein would translate yet another of Aristotle's works as well as those of some of the great Greek playwrights. It was also during this period that Abdel Aziz Fahmy[4] translated Justinian's Roman code, which forms the basis for the French legal system, indisputably the greatest in the world.

In spite of my repeated forays into these great works, every single visit to these sumptuous 'Museums of the Mind' reveals new treasures to sample. Recently, I was rereading Ahmed Loutfy El Sayed's memoirs, specifically the part where he describes his appointment as minister of education (June 1928), and I was struck by a statement stunning in its wisdom and its depth, where he writes: 'Gustave Le Bon[5] has said that the Romans during their age of decadence were more intelligent than their austere forbearers; however, they lacked the essential moral attributes such as patience, willpower, dedication, self-sacrifice and respect for law and order, all of which were behind the greatness of their forefathers.'

My own experience in life, and I stress 'in life' and not that which I have acquired from books, has led me to the conclusion that what we define as 'progress' is achieved only when these moral characteristics prevail in a society (and needless to say, in its leaders). Conversely, backwardness is the outcome of the absence of these moral attributes, even with the presence of a large segment of intelligent, well-educated people. A real move forward, or renaissance, is never achieved by intelligence or knowledge alone, but rather through the moral attributes so aptly described by Gustave Le Bon.

The preoccupation of some in the Arabic-speaking societies with fixing 'frameworks', 'systems', 'mechanisms', 'policies' and the like is indeed a noble cause, for in the current state of affairs, these are in desperate need of improvement and are in fact rife with the elements of stagnation and failure rather than those of movement and success. But this reformation, as it were, while important, can never be enough to achieve the desired objectives. What is really needed is a dedicated task force heading legislative and executive affairs; a team of tens or even hundreds of people with the essential moral qualities that Gustave Le Bon penned so astutely, and Ahmed Loutfy El Sayed stressed so insistently: patience, willpower, dedication, self-sacrifice and respect for law and order, all essential moral attributes that Gustave Le Bon pronounced as 'the secret of the greatness of their forefathers'.

Aly ibn abi-Talib (Peace be upon him) says: 'Energy and determination can revive a nation'; the reader can easily link these wise words with those of Gustave Le Bon, and see how they both lead to the same conclusion: it is the sound moral fibre of a nation that propels it forward.

THE TRUTH ABOUT 'DEMOCRACY'

A question that is the subject of intense speculation in Middle East study-centres in the United States and Europe, as well as in think tanks throughout the world, is whether the implementation of democracy in undemocratic environments could allow extremist political groups to gain a hold on power, and whether a commitment to democracy entails submitting to such an eventuality. Actually, the question betrays an all too common misconception of democracy and a poor understanding of what it really means. Democracy is a complex system that depends for its existence on three processes. The first is the arrival of the ruler in power through democratic means. The second is his exercise of power within the parameters of constitutional and legal rules and his full accountability to the people. The third is his departure from power by democratic means. These processes, which form the structural under-pinnings of any democracy, are not a function only of the ballot box, but rely essentially on civil society organizations on the one hand, and on the availability of mechanisms for democratic practices on the other. The ballot box is only a small part of a much larger whole, just one of the constituent elements of a democratic environment, which cannot exist in the absence of the three processes mentioned above, nor in the absence of the mechanisms and organizations of civil society or the institutions of democracy.

Those who are truly committed to democracy are aware of what it entails; they are working tirelessly to set in place the institutions and mechanisms for democratic political action, and to establish and con-solidate civil society institutions and organizations. The common denominator between them is institutional participation, and it is this that lays the groundwork for the three processes required for democ-racy: the ruler's accession to power by democratic means, his exercise of power by democratic means, and his departure from power by dem-ocratic means.

Then there are those who pay lip service to democracy but who see it merely as a tool they can use to reach power. Once they achieve their end, these false prophets will ride roughshod over the institutions, organizations and mechanisms of democracy, and bring the curtain down on democratic life. Actually, the only aspect of democracy they are interested in is the ballot box, which can serve as their passport to power. They know that in the context of widespread frustration at the inefficient administration of society, seething resentment at the privi-leges enjoyed by those holding a monopoly on power, and bitter anger at endemic corruption, the ballot box is likely to work in favour of those who rail against these aberrations all too common in many Third World countries – those who promise to cleanse society of the effects of these aberrations when they come to power. Of course, making promises is one thing, keeping them is quite another. In the first place, these demagogues lack the ability to introduce the required reforms; more important, they lack the will, and are more likely to destroy the components of a democratic climate than enhance them. In a way, they can be compared to the member of an orchestra who may be adept at playing his own instrument but who, on being called to conduct the full orchestra, can only produce dissonant sounds. So too with democracy, which, like an orchestra, can only function as a synergic whole – that is, if all its elements are properly brought into play. To claim that democracy can be reduced to ballot boxes in isolation from the other more important elements necessary for its existence, is both naive and dangerous.

Let us take the case of Third World countries. Most are suffering from severe political, economic, social, cultural, educational and media problems as a result of the absence of democracy, the sidelining of people with real skills, and the spread of negative values like individualism, cronyism and sycophancy. It is not by focusing exclusively on ballot boxes and their results that these societies can hope to overcome their problems; rather, they need to focus on laying down the policies and building up the organizations and mechanisms of democratic life, as well as on promoting the role of civil society. This should run in parallel with a resolute drive to introduce political, economic and educational reforms and to replace Goebbels-style media institutions with modern institutions commensurate with the requirements of the age. All these measures come under the heading of 'engineered reform', the most effective political process which can prevent chaos from setting in, or the reins of power from falling into the hands of extremist groups who will take society down a ruinous path of obscurantism, backwardness and regression. Engineered reform is guaranteed to succeed, perhaps in as little as one decade, if concerted efforts are directed at the areas mentioned above. These efforts can be summed up as follows:

- Laying down the policies and creating the mechanisms and organizations required for the conduct of democratic political action in an institutionalized fashion.
- Creating the ideal framework for the growth of civil society institutions, which are the first line of defence against fascist forces that claim to be the holders of absolute truth.
- Proceeding on the path of economic reform while never wavering from the ultimate objective of reducing the role of the state in economic life from a patriarchal role to a less intrusive role, albeit one that is decisive when it comes to laying down economic policies and guaranteeing their observance.
- Reforming educational institutions, which have sunk to abysmal standards in most countries today, producing graduates who are totally unfit to cope with the challenges of contemporary life. These educational institutions are among the worst, and the only voices

raised in their defence belong to those who contributed to their decline.

* Reforming media institutions which, in much of the Third World, continue to apply Goebbels's understanding of their role as propaganda machines serving the government, and turning them into institutions which set themselves the contemporary goal of serving the consumer.

Creating an institutional framework is thus the essential prerequisite for genuine democracy. The ballot box is but one of many links in the chain of democratic life which, if used in isolation from the other links, can become the gateway to decades of obscurantism, backwardness and repression.

In conclusion, I would like to repeat what I have said on more than one occasion. The world today knows only two models of development, progress and enlightenment in the political, economic, social, cultural, educational, and media fields. The first is the Western European model, the product of what I call a 'slow cooking' process which unfolded over more than three centuries. The other is the Asian model (Japan, Malaysia, South Korea and Singapore), the product of what I call a 'rapid cooking' process which was compressed into only a few decades. Every single country in this latter model was subjected to a concentrated dose of engineered reform, the only alternative to which is anarchy and despotism.

A. Misuse of the 'Ballot'

Adolph Hitler was born on 20 April 1889. He served as a corporal in the German army in the First World War, which ended with Germany's defeat in 1918. He spent 1920 and 1921 setting up the National Socialist Party, whose name in German forms the acronym 'Nazi'. On 30 January 1933, he was elected chancellor (prime minister). On 2 August 1934, following the death of President Paul von Hindenburg, the office of president and supreme commander was merged with that of chancellor, and Hitler assumed the title of Führer, or leader. During the 4,000 days he ruled Germany, Hitler was responsible for more deaths (conservatively estimated at 57 million) than any other individual in the history of mankind. In other words, the elections held in January 1933 and what followed in August 1934 laid the stage for the greatest human tragedy in history, in which the Holocaust is but one chapter in a series of horrific crimes against humanity. When we talk of political reform and the need for broader democracy, we would do well to heed this cautionary tale of how Hitler used the democratic process as a stepping stone to power. Thus true democracy is not a product of the ballot box alone. True, the ballot box is an essential element of democracy, but it is only a small part of a much larger whole. Democracy is a complex process made up of many elements, starting with a constitution that sets down clear mechanisms to protect democracy from its enemies, together with mechanisms and organizations to ensure the conduct of democratic political action in an institutionalized fashion. The ballot box completes the process, but if used in isolation from the other constituent elements of democracy it can produce results like those produced in Germany seventy years ago, when Adolph Hitler rode to power on the back of the ballot box.

B. Constituting Democracy

The point of departure to avoid being swept by a wave of anarchy and despotism is to adopt a modern constitution which provides for the complete separation between the different organs of the state and sets out the powers and duties of officials and the methods of calling them to account. It should also provide mechanisms for the rotation of power and safeguards to ensure that theocracies (dictatorships ruling in the name of religion) or autocracies (dictatorships ruling in the name of a specific ideology or nationalism) can never come to power. Special processes should be devised for the amendment of the constitution, and safeguards inserted to ensure that certain of its provisions are unalterable. In short, hundreds of constitutional issues need to be addressed in order to guarantee that political life proceeds in an orderly fashion in a civil society governed by the provisions of a modern constitution.

An insurmountable obstacle in the way of genuine democracy is the domination of political life by a single party, a feature that is still prevalent in a number of countries. The sidelining of other parties by the ruling party is counterproductive in that it enhances the appeal of underground movements and allows them to acquire a degree of influence far greater than they would otherwise have had.

C. Consolidating Human Rights

Building a real and vibrant democratic life entails devising a detailed plan to consolidate civil society in general and human rights organizations in particular, as these are among the most effective mechanisms which can prevent anti-democratic parties or movements from taking advantage of the democratic system to reach influential positions. Unfortunately, the bureaucracies in certain political systems that are in the early stages of democratic transformation are hostile to civil society organizations, even though they are the main bulwark in the face of takeovers by anti-democratic forces.

It is important in this connection to realize that there is a vast difference between the real popularity of a certain trend, and the apparent popularity it can appear to have under certain circumstances. For example, a trend could gain as much as 60 per cent of the vote in the context of voter apathy, such as when a silent majority of the electorate stays away from the polls because it believes its participation will make no difference. If this silent majority was to participate, the popularity of that same trend could drop to less than half that percentage. It is not difficult to understand the indifference behind poor election turnouts; political apathy can be attributed to a widespread sense of the futility of participation. Overcoming the problem does not require centuries or even decades: all it takes is a moment of truth to replace people's negative attitudes towards participation with feelings of confidence that the election process is not merely a charade, and that their participation can make a difference. Poor voter turnout needs to be addressed qualitatively, not quantitatively.

D. Models of Democracy

Before talking of political reform, we also need to recognize that the world today knows only two models of development in general, and of development in a democratic environment in particular: the former is the Western European/North American model and the latter is the Asian model in countries such as Singapore, Taiwan, South Korea and Malaysia. In some of the talks I gave, as mentioned previously, I used the expressions 'slow cooking' to describe the process of development which unfolded over centuries in Western Europe and North America, and 'rapid cooking' to describe that process in the case of the Asian model, where it was compressed into a few decades. If Arabs want to see their countries attain the level of progress, development, prosperity, stability democracy and general freedoms to which they aspire, within the time-frame of a few years rather than over centuries, they need to draw the necessary lessons from the Asian examples, whose adoption of democracy was dictated by internal factors, and not by external pressure. In all the successful Asian experiments, society passed through a stage in which the main focus was on economic success. This went hand in hand with the growth and expansion of the middle class, which usually results in a higher level of democracy.

E. Specificity of the Democratic Process

In recent years, the issue of internal political reform has come to be associated with an external factor that needs to be addressed very seriously. I am talking of the way certain great powers take it upon themselves not only to call for political reforms in other countries, but even sometimes to apply pressure on those countries to introduce certain reforms. It is important for both sides to realize that the boundary between asking and demanding must not be crossed, and that moving from a stage of recommending reforms to one of applying pressure on a country to force it to comply is at best useless, and at worst counterproductive. From my first-hand experience in the world of management, where I have been actively involved at both the executive and academic levels for many years, I know that any real constructive change can only be brought about by believers, and not by followers. As this principle applies in the world of management, so too does it apply in the world of politics, and to relations between nations. In other words, all that an outside party is entitled to do is to request and persuade; the use of coercion rather than persuasion is self-defeating. Not only will it fail to produce the desired result but, more often than not, it will actually produce the opposite result. If we analyze the experience of the Asian Tigers,[6] which are now enjoying real democracy, we find that there is not one case among them in which change and development came about in response to external pressure.

EGYPT AS AN EXAMPLE OF THE ARABIC-SPEAKING SOCIETIES

1. Change and Stability

There have been many indications recently that the Egyptian administration has come to realize the failure of the policies that have governed its economic and political life since the late 1950s and through the 1960s. I am referring specifically to the policies limiting the role of the private sector and reducing areas of cooperation with multinational companies, and to those governing agriculture, industry, housing and education – policies to which all of Egypt's major problems can be traced.

But while recognizing that no cure is possible without radical reform, the administration believes that any change has to consider the requirements of political and social stability. Several serious incidents have made the situation even more sensitive and complex: the 1977 riots,[7] the assassination of President Sadat,[8] and the workers' strike at the Helwan steel mills in 1987. As we consider how to balance the inevitability of change with the imperative need for stability, we would do well to keep a popular Egyptian adage in mind: 'He whose hand is in water is not like he whose hand is in fire.'

While it is natural for all the opposition wings to favour change, it is equally natural for the ruling administration to be more concerned with stability. The focus in the opposition press has always been on the need for change, regardless of how it might affect stability, and political and social security. The Tagamu' Party[9] call for changes which are in line with its ideology, namely changes of a socialist nature. The Wafd Party[10] is aimed at changes of a liberal nature, based on the amendment of the constitution in the direction of political liberalization. The Labour Party is clamouring for changes that remain undefined, even in the minds of its leaders, whose orientations have become more obscure than ever, following the recent merger between these successors of the old fascist party, Jeune Egypte,[11] the Liberal Party, the Socialist Party and the Moslem Brotherhood. As fervently as it reiterates the need for change (of whatever nature), the opposition remains curiously silent about the need to effect change in a way that would not jeopardize political and social stability, and plunge Egypt into the anarchy raging through the Middle East today. There are, as we all know, a number of regional and global parties with an interest in keeping the political pot on the boil in various parts of the world, and they would not be averse to seeing a similar situation erupt in Egypt.

An observer confronted with the two positions may wonder where the truth lies – in the over-sensitivity to and awareness of security requirements, or in the relentless call for change. Actually, both positions contain a modicum of truth. But to date, none of the opposition parties have come up with concrete proposals for change. They have stuck to generalities and catch cries, disregarding the effects of change on stability, and forgetting that, as an opposition, they have never been involved in any form of administrative government. With the exception of the Wafd Party, all the factions of the Egyptian opposition share a common past: totalitarianism, fascism or theocracy. With such a legacy, is it any wonder that their strident calls for change should blithely disregard the disastrous consequences of instituting change without careful planning? There was an opposition party that could have formed an objective and balanced counterpoise to the party in power had it not, regrettably, fallen under the influence of one man's overriding ambition, a man whose race against time is doomed to fail.[12]

These reservations on the opposition's attitude to change do not imply unqualified support for the administration's excessively cautious position in this respect. Although it is wise to aim for change without affecting political and social stability, any error in timing could cause the foundations of security to crack and upset stability. Time is not an ally for anyone called upon to tackle the massive problems of contemporary Egypt. On the contrary, it can work against him and hinder the possibility of reaching comprehensive solutions to the country's chronic problems.

In other words, while it is right to insist on maintaining security and stability when contemplating changes in political and economic orientations in matters as important as education, industry, agriculture and housing, it is equally true that to postpone instituting the necessary changes is to jeopardize stability.

Let us turn to a notorious historical example of the fatal consequences of indecision. Had the French monarchy in 1789 not refused to institute the democratic reforms to which the French people aspired, had Louis XVI sided with the Commons and not with the Nobles during the constitutional crisis, the French Revolution may not have taken place and the monarchy may have survived, as did its counterpart in England. Scores of examples attest to the validity of the dictum that to postpone taking action may itself be twice as dangerous as the immediate tackling of problems, however intractable they seem to be. Yet Egypt today is treated to the spectacle of armchair critics loudly denouncing any attempt to change systems which have become enshrined idols protected by a clergy whose members jealously guard their privileges.

2. The Need for Change

A. Public Life. Most Egyptians today agree that there is an urgent need to bring about fundamental changes in public life, and that this is a prerequisite for raising standards of living in the country. This is the theme of an ongoing national dialogue, about which there is a general consensus. It develops into a debate when people – those in public life and private citizens alike – suggest how best to achieve this.

It should be noted, however, that the nature of this 'consensus' has changed in recent years. Thirty years ago, it was still generally believed that the country had to overcome the disastrous defeat it suffered in the 1967 War against Israel,[13] and regain the territories seized by Israel at that time. Even ten years ago, the national mood was still strongly marked by the trauma of 1967, holding the Egyptians hostage to the past. Moreover, the then-prevailing world order also helped keep the national debate mired in the rhetoric of the past, specifically in the time-worn and cliché-ridden slogans of the 1950s and 1960s.

Today the inner maturity of the Egyptians, together with the new conditions in the world, have liberated their thinking somewhat. Most of them now realize that those old slogans were not matched in reality and that neither the Egypt of the 1960s nor of the 1970s responded to the aspirations of its citizens. In addition, the collapse of the citadels of socialism revealed the utter failure of that movement, whether in its political, economic or social form, to bring affluence and social justice for any of the societies which espoused it. These factors led the Egyptians to break out of their stereotyped thinking of the past, and the collective will for change has come to be informed by the following considerations:

- Change must come about through a process of gradual reform, not in revolutionary upheavals. The experience of many countries over the last fifty years has convinced wide sections of the Egyptian population that the 'revolutionary' path invariably fails to attain the desired goals, not least because power usually ends up in the hands of people who lack leadership qualities and who have neither the experience nor the vision required to lead their countries to a better future.
- Change should not be instituted according to an ideological agenda. Ideology, which dominated the world for a century-and-a-half, was discredited in the last decade of the twentieth century, and promises to remain so for a long time to come.
- Change should be directed in the first instance at achieving economic growth by providing a climate in which the tools and mechanisms of the economy can operate effectively.

Thus, the consensus for change extends also to an agreement over the modalities of how to achieve it. With the exception of a few fringe – albeit dangerous – groups, most Egyptians believe change can best come about through reform, not revolution, and that reform should be instituted according to pragmatic, not ideological, considerations. This is particularly true for economic reforms, which will in turn entail reforms in the political system.

To further probe whether Egyptians agree on the nature and direction of the required changes, we must first cast a look at today's world and how it has changed since the Second World War:

- Since the demise of the Soviet Union, we now have the group of advanced Western nations, led by the United States as the sole superpower at the summit of the world community.
- The economic bankruptcy of the Eastern bloc brought with it the

complete collapse of the ideology to which this bloc subscribed.
* The Cold War is well and truly over, and thus, so is the need for a bloc calling itself the 'non-aligned movement'.
* The world now recognizes that a society's progress and its ability to overcome economic crises is contingent on its ability to diffuse the spirit and dynamics of private enterprise among its citizens – that this is the only path to economic success, prosperity and progress.

And so, humankind bade farewell to the twentieth century with a global rationale that had nothing to do with that which prevailed for the two decades following the Second World War, and even less to do with that found in the early 1900s. In the new rationale, the choices are simple. Socialism in all its forms has been relegated to the realm of history; it is no longer a viable option for the future. Only two options remain: either to lurch along without a clear sense of direction, or to address the world's problems purposefully through the mechanisms of the new rationale, which are linked to the dynamics of market economy, to democracy and to human rights.

Experts on Third World issues believe developing countries' prospects for socio-economic growth will improve in direct proportion to the rate at which they proceed to apply these mechanisms. The enormous problems facing most Third World countries are time bombs waiting to go off, and any hesitation could prove fatal. At best, countries that procrastinate will lag further and further behind in the race for progress; at worst, they will implode, with dire consequences for their own people and for the world at large.

In addition to embarking on the process of reform, some countries can capitalize on their geopolitical importance to speed it up. Egypt is a good example. As it stands poised to shift from a present fraught with problems to a future filled with hope, it must be realized that Egypt will need more than ideas to safely navigate the choppy waters separating the two. In the new global rationale, it can invest its unique geopolitical status to promote internal development and thus defuse what is rapidly becoming a crisis situation. At this stage in its history, Egypt stands at the junction of three paths. One will lead to the perpetuation of the status quo, the second to still further decline, and the third to a solution of its problems, to progress and prosperity in the context of social peace and political stability. Access to the third path is contingent on devising a mechanism by which to effect the desired changes.

The problem in Egypt is that it continues to insist on using the wrong sort of people. To begin with, the political leadership must act decisively to remove from the arena of public life those officials who are evidently unable to perform at the required standard of excellence. According to scholars of constitutional law in Western societies, democracy can only be built by democrats. By the same token, a better future for Egypt can only be built by those of its citizens who have proved their competence and dedication to the governing principles of the new era, namely, the importance of human resources and a belief in the efficiency of a market economy, the merits of modern management and marketing sciences.

The real crisis does not lie in a lack of qualified people but, rather, in the absence of such people from the public arena over the last forty years, while others who were not necessarily the most efficient, experienced, honest, intelligent or successful Egyptians dominated. Egypt is one of the rare Third World countries blessed with a huge pool of talented people who are more than capable of efficiently and loyally running its public life. However, most are excluded from this arena because they display characteristics that are out of tune with the system in force, which is based on loyalty to a select group of individuals, the same people who have the monopoly on public posts in the state bureaucracy. Any talk of reform as meaning the implementation of better ideas – not the use of better people to achieve that – will remain no more than talk until the system wakes up and allows new ideas to pervade it.

B. Housing. One system that needs to be changed, and without further delay, is that of housing. The most critical aspect of the housing problem in Egypt is the enormous discrepancy between dwindling supply and burgeoning demand. In the late 1950s and through the 1960s, the state enacted laws which served to deter the private sector from investing in the construction of housing units, particularly those for rent. Faced with an alarming drop in the number of rentals, the state was forced to step into the housing market to meet the demand, which was growing as fast as the population.

The state, of course, failed to satisfactorily perform the task it had set itself, not because of any inherent failing but because it is impossible for a state to accomplish such a formidable task. The only practical solution is to repeal the housing laws that created the imbalance between supply and demand in the first place. The problem will not disappear through such palliatives as prohibiting the sale of apartments, key money, or rent advances. Moreover, the longer the waiting, the more acute the disparity will become between the demand for and the supply of housing units. As the disparity grows, so too does the pressure of the housing problem on society's nervous system, pressure which is growing more intolerable. Eventually, the strains and stresses of the situation may cause cracks in the foundations of political and social stability and security.

C. Agriculture. The agricultural problem is another example that shows Egypt's need for change. Agriculture is the mode of production most closely associated with the idea of private initiative, in the sense that it epitomizes more clearly than any other the organic link between private initiative, as represented in an individual's direct personal interest in the success of a private venture, and the overall success of this mode of production. In the area of agriculture, the concept of private property is more firmly entrenched than in any other sphere of production. This is why agriculture succeeds brilliantly under systems which encourage private ownership, and which recognize that individual creativity stemming from personal interest fuels productivity and success. Agricultural production in the US, Canada, France, Germany and France is a success story. In the socialist countries, it suffers greatly from the lack of enthusiasm of farm workers, from low productivity and from visible degradation. If we compare Algeria and Morocco – two adjoining countries with nearly identical geographic and demographic conditions but with different political systems – we see that in the former, a socialist state, agricultural production is a complete failure, whereas in Morocco, with its free system of agricultural production, this sector is highly successful.

In Egypt the system is mixed and highly intricate. The general framework is socialist, based on severe limitations of agricultural land holdings, and a legal system that has transformed the landlord into a hired hand and made the tenant farmer the real owner. Moreover, a large number of agricultural products, some of them strategic, must be sold to the government. The problem, of course, is that any attempt to reform will necessarily entail changes that could affect political and social stability. But failure to act would be even worse. Postponing the necessary decisions could only lead to the further degradation of agricultural productivity and increasing tension between the parties concerned. As agricultural production drops and the demographic explosion continues to send ever-widening ripples through society, the state will be subjected to enormous pressure to provide large amounts of foreign currency to import more and more food.

D. Soldiers' Living Conditions. Another example of the importance of timely decisions is the mutiny of the Central Security Forces in

February 1986. The spark that ignited the incident was the deplorable living conditions of the soldiers. Had a decision been taken in time to improve their conditions, there would have been no mutiny and the agents provocateurs would have remained silent.

Countless examples show that the dangers inherent in delaying the adoption of decisions concerning crucial problems far outweigh any short-lived continuity and stability that ignoring the problems can provide. In conclusion, it can be said that the real difficulty lies not in having to choose between change and stability but in coming to realize that both factors are necessary: change for the better while ensuring stability and fulfilling security needs.

RIGHTS AND DUTIES

A conversation which took place years ago with Desmond Stewart, a British writer known for his love and appreciation of Egypt and the Egyptian people, served as the inspiration for this chapter. The author of such works as *Great Cairo: Mother of the World* and *The Men of Friday*,[14] Stewart had very definite views on the distinctive traits of the contemporary Egyptian personality. I recall that one of his most perceptive observations was that an enormous discrepancy has grown in the two decades of autocratic rule since 1952 between the Egyptians' sense of right and their sense of duty.

If the blame for Egypt's present situation lies squarely with the government, this does not mean that the responsibility of Egyptians as individuals should be overlooked, particularly regarding duties and rights. Rather, there is a connection between the government's attitudes and performance level, and those of the Egyptian citizen towards his/her rights and duties.

It should be stressed that it is as a result of the government's shoddy performance and its poor record that most Egyptians have become passive citizens who are unduly conscious of their rights and privileges – not least in the area of pensions – without developing a corresponding sense of obligation. A typical Egyptian citizen is greatly concerned with his/her right to public employment and its many benefits. Then there is his/her right to obtain housing, through the government if possible; followed by his/her right to a job abroad – preferably on secondment from the government; his/her right to go on pilgrimage to Mecca; to buy subsidized food and clothing, and so on through an endless list of state-supported privileges. Never will an Egyptian citizen display a sense of obligation similar to that of, say, his/her German counterpart, who is fully aware

that to enjoy the privileges of citizenship, he/she must first perform
such basic duties as actively participating in his/her country's production process, protecting his/her environment, and contributing towards
solving society's problems by giving serious thought to their causes
and their possible solutions.

The Egyptian president once spoke of the need for a 'great awakening' in the life of all Egyptians. This is certainly true. Moreover, unless
there is such an awakening – and soon – Egypt is heading towards certain disaster. But the question is: what does the president mean by
'awakening'? Does he mean that the government should waken from
the deep sleep into which it has been plunged by three decades of totalitarian rule, never guided by the lights of freedom and democracy? Or
does he mean the awakening of the people to the duties and obligations
incumbent on them, which they neglected for many years while claiming their right to the material advantages provided by the state, never
attempting to expand the circle of rights to encompass political issues
such as the right to influence fateful decisions, the right to choose leaders freely or, at the very least, the right to live in a twenty-first-century
environment where roads and basic public services are concerned? Or
did the president mean an awakening of both government and citizens?

I believe the call for a 'great awakening' cannot become a reality
unless it is directed first at the government and the administration, and
only then at the citizens of Egypt, in order to rouse them from a slum-
ber so aptly described half a century ago by the poet who lamented:

> The great Pharaohs shuddered and recoiled, aghast
> To see such heritage go to waste.
> They saw a nation lag behind its age
> That once had always had the lead.
> I almost hear the echo of their cry
> Across the centuries to be heard:
> Sons of Egypt! Hear our voice!
> Life or Death, this is the choice
> And nothing in between.[15]

The awakening of the government will come about on the day it
acknowledges that the situation in Egypt has sunk to an all-time low,
in all areas and at all levels, because of its own political and economic
policies. The government must also admit that the time for stop-gap
repairs is long gone, and that nothing short of a radical shift in those
policies can save Egypt.

At the same time the awakening of the Egyptian citizens requires a rekindling of the flame of positive nationalism in their hearts and minds, which can transform them from being interested solely in rights and benefits, to being mindful of their duties to society and to the nation. A citizen who accepts the state as a father figure, responsible for providing his/her children with education, employment and all their other needs, is a negative citizen, even though he/she was moulded so by years of oppression which stripped him/her of his/her will and the spirit of endeavour.

There is no doubt that the transformation of Egyptians into 'hirelings' of the regime, wholly dependent on it for their livelihood – and for all the aspects of their life – was a deliberate policy of Egypt's rulers from the 1950s to the 1960s, designed to help them consolidate their grip on power. In this way, they succeeded in suppressing all opposition; an entire people succumbed.

But there is more than one way to rekindle the spirit of nationalism and a sense of civic duty. The first is by setting an example. When people see their leaders not practising what they preach, they become alienated: their values are shaken and their sense of duty to society and to the nation recedes. Very few of the players on the stage of Egyptian public life can be held up as examples of exceptional competence or as paragons of intelligence, knowledge and culture. Indeed, many display only modest abilities, mediocre intelligence and little culture. Worse, they often blatantly lack the qualities and moral virtue associated with leadership. Needless to say, the absence of these elements in so many of Egypt's public personalities does not bode well for the prospects of change. The double standards to which the Egyptian people have for so long been exposed has quite understandably made them cynical and filled with bitterness. They need to see their rulers set an example, from the president down.

The roots of the problem go back to the political climate which prevailed in Egypt in the 1950s and 1960s, when individual freedom and independent thought were suppressed, ostensibly in the name of social cohesion but in actual fact as a means of controlling society. At every level in the chain of command, superiors were obeyed without question, and obsequiousness and sycophancy were de rigueur. This is the school from which many of the Egyptian functionaries graduated. Today's requirements make it imperative to hand the reins of public life over to people who derive their value systems from different sources.

The Egyptian young people cannot be blamed for losing faith in a value system which allows inept and second-rate people to attain leading positions, and where success is more often than not due less to competency than to shameful practices or personal relations. The years-long absence of good examples was not the result of a divine curse or historical accident but stemmed from a deliberate attempt to eliminate independent thinkers and people of integrity from the public arena. The suppression and control characteristic of the last forty years, in which most officials surrounded themselves exclusively with 'yes-men', sadly explains the disappearance of good examples and the propagation of the mediocrity we know so well. We cannot ask Egyptian young people to believe in or to accept this any longer.

The second way to rekindle the spirit of nationalism and a sense of civic duty is by eliciting the help of the mass media, but of media that are free, not that cater to the interests of specific persons or tendencies. Egyptians are bitterly resentful of the opportunism that has characterized their mass media for the past thirty years. The newspapers, radio and television have all, under a series of directors who were no more than lackeys of the totalitarian regime and the secret services, become what they are today: repetitive and dull.

The third way is through educational institutions, at both school and university levels, for these can infuse young learners with a true and effective nationalist spirit, based on love of country and a strong sense of civic duty, not a superficial love expressed in the rote chanting of sentimental anthems. While there is a pressing need for a complete overhaul of the educational system to bring it in line with the requirements of the age, it is imperative to embark on any process of reform by first defining the long-term goals of the educational process in Egypt in a strategic paper, and then designing the programmes by which these goals can be reached at the level of curricula, teachers, students and schools. This is the only way not only to ensure the formation of modern citizens who are creative, committed and competitive, but also to solve a long list of problems which, though apparently unrelated to the issue of education, are in fact organically linked to it.

The fourth way is through mosque and church, where religious leaders should understand that their duty, apart from teaching the precepts of the faith, is not to preach hatred of others or incite extremist ideas but, rather, to instil a profound sense of duty to society and teach that work is sacred. Egyptian Moslems are Moslems in their own manner: Egypt's Islam has been imbued with the country's historical characteristics of tolerance and coexistence between different faiths.

Literature and the arts offer a fifth way to inspire a civic spirit. Literature is the conscience of the nation, and many a nation has risen from ruin thanks to great literature. Voltaire, Rousseau, Montesquieu and Diderot can proudly claim to have inspired public freedom and democracy in the West. Unfortunately, in Egypt, more than five decades of hypocrisy by a large number of kowtowing intellectuals and writers, who turned a blind eye to all forms of oppression, have caused Egyptian art and literature to lose their credibility among vast sectors of the Egyptian people.

Opposition groups too have an important role to play in this connection. But unless the opposition ceases to incite and to insult, its ability to nurture a sense of civic duty in the people will remain very limited. The opposition will lose its credibility as a seeker of reform and will be seen, instead, as aiming to settle personal scores, or to reach powerful positions. Little has changed since Sa'd Zaghloul described the opposition thus: 'To them the insults, and to us the seats in parliament.' The Egyptian opposition, as a whole, is in dire need of objectivity and seriousness. That is particularly true of the Left which, more than other wings, needs to pause and reflect to ensure that it is not held accountable for the demagogical trend prevailing in many ranks of the political opposition in Egypt today.

President Mubarak's administration should make more effort to respond to the wishes of the opposition, especially since it is generally acknowledged that it is far more representative at the popular level (particularly the Wafd, Labour and Tagamu' Parties) than the number of seats it holds in the People's Assembly would indicate. The administration is surely aware that those parties have behind them more than 50 per cent of Egyptian public opinion, and that at least half the country's intellectuals and educated people support them. Thus, a positive response by the presidency to the opposition's demands would help generate a sense of civic duty on its part. There must be many issues on which Mubarak's administration and the most cultured and enlightened groups of Egyptians – more than half of whom are represented by the three parties in question – could see eye to eye. Among such issues is the opposition's desire to amend the system of election to the People's Assembly, as well as its demand that the president should relinquish the chairmanship of his political party. The opposition also believes that the regime should abstain from giving unconditional support to some of its public figures, and that the head of state should be chosen through direct general elections rather than through a public referendum on a sole candidate nominated by the Assembly.

It is worth mentioning that the reaction of the so-called 'national' press to the president's call for a 'great awakening' does not augur well for its chances of successfully drumming up enthusiasm for such a goal. The hypocritical reaction of the state's eminent writers and editors may well have a negative impact on the citizens, who have long lost faith in the sycophantic national press.

Moreover, the media have taken the president's call to mean the awakening of the citizens alone, whereas observers are unanimous in believing that the awakening should be, first and foremost, that of the government, since the present lethargy of the citizens is but a reaction to the failure of successive governments, a form of passive self-defence, as it were. Where are the eminent writers who insist that there can be no great awakening if the president himself does not recognize the sorry state that Egypt has come to? Yet the government and all its men and institutions never publicly admit the dim situation, nor will they admit the grave errors and failed policies committed against the country over decades – in the economy, agriculture, education, the public sector, the military establishment, and so on.

Real confidence-building measures are required to win the public back, in all spheres. Without the growth and development of a sense of duty towards Egypt in the government and among its citizens, the 'great awakening' which is necessary to pull Egypt out of its present slump will remain no more than a dream. With the enforcement of this sense of duty, the capacity for finding and working on solutions for the problems obstructing the development of progress in Egypt will prevail.

NOTES

1. (1868–1932). Egyptian poet and dramatist; one of the pioneers of the Egyptian literary movement; he owes the title of 'amir al shu'ara" (prince of the poets) to his distinctive prominent poetry.
2. (1872–1963). Egyptian intellectual known for his anti-colonial activism; also reform rector of Cairo University.
3. (1889–1973). The greatest Arab writer and intellectual in the twentieth century. Although he was blind, he enlightened the hearts of the sons and daughters of the Arabic-speaking societies, until they opted for an atavistic and backward path. His book *The Wednesday Talk* was written in three volumes, published in Cairo in 1925, 1926 and 1945 respectively. Most of the third volume was published as articles in the newspaper *Al Syassa* in 1923, prior to their compilation into a book in 1945.
4. A star of the liberal era of modern Egypt who was the father of the text of the Egyptian Constitution of 1923 and who was the first Egyptian judge to head Egypt's Cour de Cassation; he was known in the 1940s for his call to write Arabic with Latin alphabet, similar to what Kamal Ataturk had implemented in Turkey in the 1920s.
5. (1841–1931). French psychologist, sociologist and physicist; his works include theories on race, behaviour, and crowd psychology.
6. The Asian Tigers are the societies such as Singapore, South Korea, Hong Kong that remarkably flourished economically during the 1980s and 1990s, and therefore realized unprecedented states of welfare in a number of Asian countries.
7. Following President Sadat's visit to Israel.
8. Occurred during a victory parade, on 6 October 1981 by Islamic militants belonging to the Jihad group.

9. Major Egyptian leftist (socialist) political party; calls for the original principles of the 1952 revolution.
10. Political party founded in Egypt by Sa'd Zaghloul in 1919.
11. An Egyptian fascist movement inspired by the rise of Mussolini in Italy and Adolf Hitler in Germany. It became a political society in the early 1930s under the leadership of Ahmed Hussein.
12. Fouad Serag-Eddin, who was a key political figure in pre-1952 Egypt and who caused the Egyptian Christians/Copts to flee the Wafd Party twice: in 1943, when he was behind the dismissal of the party's number two leader, Makram Ebeid (a national hero and a Copt), and once again in 1984 when he embarked on an alliance with the Muslim Brothers.
13. The war between Israel and its Arab neighbours – Egypt, Jordan and Syria – waged between 5 and 10 June 1967. As a consequence, the Arab states lost to Israel's control the Sinai Peninsula and the Gaza Strip, the entire West Bank of the Jordan River (including East Jerusalem), and the Golan Heights. During the period preceding the war the already tense relations between the sides deteriorated over the continuing actions of Palestinian guerrillas against Israel, the strengthening of the Palestinian national movement, and the dispute over utilization of the waters of the Jordan River. The situation was exacerbated by the signing of the Egyptian–Syrian Joint Defence Agreement in November 1967, the Israeli shooting down of a Syrian aircraft (April 1967) and erroneous Soviet reports of an Israeli amassment of troops in the Golan Heights. Friction peaked when, on 18 May, complying with Egyptian demands the UN withdrew its forces from the Sinai Peninsula. This was followed by the arrival of large numbers of Egyptian forces in the Peninsula. The Egyptians imposed a blockade over Israeli navigation in the Gulf of Aqaba (21 May) and signed defence agreements with Jordan (30 May) and Iraq (3 June). On the morning of 5 June, Israel launched a large-scale air strike, practically destroying the air forces of all Arab countries involved, and thus began the war. Apart from the territorial losses, Egypt saw most of its army destroyed in the fighting and its hegemony in the Arab world greatly weakened. The defeat also affected the regime, causing the resignation of President Gamal Abd Al-Nasser, which he retracted twenty-four hours later. Another of its important results was the adoption of Resolution 242 by the UN Security Council, which called for an Israeli withdrawal from occupied lands in return for peace and Arab recognition.
14. Desmond Stewart, *Great Cairo: Mother of the World* (London: Rupert Hart-Davis, 1969) and *The Men of Friday* (London: Heinemann, 1961).
15. Abbas el Aqqad, a well-known Egyptian thinker, writer and poet, born in Aswan in 1889; died in Cairo on 12 March 1964.

8

Economic Progress

So far I have addressed the issue of reform only in its political sense, not in its economic one. Economic reform (which is distinct from fiscal reform) is, on the one hand, the product of political reform and, on the other, that of an economic environment, as well as of an investment climate attractive to foreign capital and to international and local projects. There has been a great deal of irresponsible talk by armchair economists on what economic reform entails. Actually, the issue of economic reform must be seen from the perspective of modern management science, which teaches us that what cannot be measured cannot be appraised. Today there is a whole branch of management science dealing with this question. Originally established under the name 'Performance Evaluation', it is now known simply as 'Benchmark'. The importance of this branch lies in its complete disregard of subjective factors like emotions, instincts, aspirations, whims and ideological inclinations, in favour of objective measurement criteria or benchmarks. It would take hundreds of pages to explain the use of benchmarks in measuring economic performance, so I will limit myself to citing a couple of examples here:

- The volume of direct foreign investment in Egypt in any of the recent years (2008, for example) amounted to a paltry 1.5 billion US dollars, which is half the amount invested by any international oil company in east Russia on a single oilfield, and less than 3 per cent of foreign investments in Malaysia during the same year.
- Egypt's textile exports account for less than 15 to 20 per cent of the potential of this sector, as determined by extremely reliable international studies. At the same time, the textile exports of a smaller country, Jordan, exceed those of Egypt.

SUCCESS OR FAILURE OF ECONOMIC REFORM

Experiments in economic reform have been seen in a number of countries over the last twenty-five years. In some cases the experiments achieved impressive results, while in many others they failed. Somewhere in between stands a third group of countries, those which made significant headway at first only to suffer setbacks further down the road.

In my opinion the experiments which succeeded – and sustained their momentum – were those which did not address the process of reform from a purely economic perspective. After all, economic ideas, systems, structures and mechanisms (usually the creation of economists – who are usually academicians) cannot, in and of themselves, guarantee consistent and sustained success. Certainly the economists play a vital role, for without them the process of economic reform cannot be initiated in the first place: they are the ones who determine the framework for monetary reform followed by economic reform; but this represents only the first stage.

In order to better illustrate this point, let us draw a parallel here between the first stage of economic reform and the construction of a state-of-the-art sports complex. Once the sports complex has been built and fitted out in accordance with the required specifications, the role of the architect and contractor ends, and that of the managers, administrators and players begins. However well designed such a complex may be, it cannot in itself guarantee a brilliant record of achievement. The same applies to the planning of monetary and economic reform. Though a vital and indispensable element of any reform programme, the planning (admittedly a difficult and complex task) is merely the first stage in a longer process. In the next stage the economists must stand back to allow the managers and administrators – and players – to take over.

In fact, the reason behind the failure of some economic reform programmes is that they remained under the control of the economists-academicians longer than they should have. Conversely, the experiments which enjoyed the highest and most consistent rate of success are those in which the planners handed over the reins of control at the right time to a cadre of dynamic, talented and qualified management executives who then implemented the reforms.

As to the countries whose economic reform programmes got off to a good start but faltered later, I believe that this was due to the absence of clear lines of demarcation between the role of the economists as planners, and that of the cadre of top management executives who are required to put the programme into effect. The overlapping of the two roles beyond the take-off stage caused some economic reform programmes to suffer the setbacks and reversals that they did, though in some cases these have been depicted as far worse than they really were. For example, the setback faced by the Asian Tigers after the initial brilliant success of their economic reform programmes, although serious, was not devastating. In fact, many of them were expected to overcome the crisis before the millennium. They can draw on the inspiring experience of Mexico, which made a complete recovery from its economic crisis thanks to its excellent cadre of administrators and management executives.

My view, then, is that prolonging the stage of monetary and economic reform in which academe-oriented economists are in the driver's seat can lead to many problems and reversals. Once the initial phase has begun, the focus must shift from the structural aspect of monetary and economic reform to the practical aspects of administration, modern management systems, marketing strategies and human resources, with particular emphasis on the cadre of leaders in the field of executive management – including the field of marketing, arguably the most important area of modern economic life.

Shifting the focus from the planning stage to the execution stage is extremely difficult, and usually involves a power struggle, possibly an all-out showdown, between the adherents of different schools of thought: one whose experience lies in the past and the other which has its eye on the future. There is no doubt that a speedy resolution of the conflict in favour of the modern school is one of the keys to sustainable economic success that is less susceptible to setbacks and regressions.

Finally, the long-term sustainability of reform programmes can only be guaranteed if a number of basic principles are observed. The economic reform experiments which achieved the highest rate of sustained success are those which believed that the private sector should play a pivotal role in economic life and that the views of the business sector should be taken into account without, however, allowing that sector to actively participate in the policy-making process. For here arises the danger of conflict of interests: business people by their very nature have only short-term or, at best, medium-term interests, while those concerning society must be long-term. This makes it imperative to have another level – a contemporary political cadre which might comprise top management executives but certainly not businessmen – that can strike a balance between the short and long-term interests.

THE EGYPTIAN ECONOMY: AN EXAMPLE OF THE ARABIC-SPEAKING COUNTRIES

1. Egypt's Economic Conditions

During some twenty meetings, lectures, round-table discussions and television interviews, I was asked about the economic situation in Egypt, and my reply was the following:

- Before 1952, there was a thriving middle class in Egypt which somehow managed to be both Egyptian and cosmopolitan, traditional and modern, at one and the same time. But it was a class limited in size, which meant that it was unable to sustain Egypt's liberal experiment in the political, economic and social spheres.
- The public sector experiment failed in Egypt for the same reason it failed in every single country that adopted it, namely that the public sector produces administrators as opposed to managers. The difference between the two is the difference between administrative affairs and economic management. The establishment of a giant factory is not an aim in itself; the aim is that it should be economically successful. The public sector experiment proved that expressions like 'political viability' and 'social viability' are misleading, and that any project, however politically and socially viable it may purport to be, will collapse if it does not meet the criteria of economic feasibility.
- The transition from a socialist-inspired command economy to a free market economy was carried out rather haphazardly in the 1970s. The groundwork for a smooth transition was not properly laid, and the task was not entrusted to those best equipped to perform it, namely, a cadre of efficient modern managers.
- The years between 1981 and 1991 were given over to infrastructural projects whose execution required massive outlays of money, time and energy, without this being reflected in economic indicators.
- 1991 to 1997 saw the introduction of extensive fiscal reforms which, together with a moderate degree of economic reform, made for a relative improvement in the investment climate, which was reflected in positive economic indicators.
- 1997 to 2000 saw the emergence of problems and difficulties, the significance of which must neither be downplayed nor overstated. One such problem was that the process of economic reform was not accompanied by a process of reform in the management structure based on a methodological plan designed to reduce the role of the state in size, while expanding it in importance. The role of the state should focus on laying down policies and following up their implementation in a spirit compatible with the ideal role of the state as envisaged by German Chancellor Konrad

Adenauer in the early 1950s, namely to serve as a social compass for society.

There was also the problem of poor credit lending, a problem which cannot be solved through launching defamatory campaigns against suspected malefactors or throwing them in prison, unless of course there is clear evidence that a crime was in fact committed. Problems of this kind are not unique to Egypt, but have plagued many other countries, including some of the most advanced in the world, which have managed to solve them through banking procedures rather than media blitzes and police arrests.

It also became obvious during the same period that the regulatory framework governing the investment climate needed to be further streamlined, with a view to ultimately creating an investor-friendly climate akin to the Dubai model. Then there was the question of national mega-projects which were exacting such a heavy toll on national resources that there was talk of abandoning them. While these projects do pose a problem, I believe that scrapping them altogether would be an unnecessarily extreme measure, and that a way should be found of pushing ahead with their completion in different forms that can reduce the burden they are placing on the state treasury.

In short, there are problems that it would be as inappropriate to liken them to a cancer as to a slight cold; problems that are an inevitable by-product of any economic reform programme. All are curable, even the problem of outstanding debt payments.

I always end my comments on the economic situation in Egypt with the words of the distinguished economics professor and former member of the Shura Council, Dr Adel Bishay,[1] who believes that solutions to current economic problems lie in the field of management, not in economics, and who recommends that they be inspired by advanced management techniques rather than devised by professors of economics.

2. Work: A Forgotten 'Art'

We were out somewhere in the middle of Egypt's sandy Western Desert, south of the Qattara Depression and north of the Great Sea of Sand, when my companion, one of the three top personalities in the international oil industry, said, 'In my view, the Egyptian authorities and people are making a mistake when they attribute current economic problems to a lack of potential or natural resources. In fact, Egypt is rich in both; what it lacks is another vital element – work!' He paused for a moment, then added:

You know how much I love Egypt and how badly I want to see its economy thrive, yet I must tell you that because of the political situation over the past thirty years, you have lost the 'art of work', and without that, you cannot hope to make progress. I recently went through some reports by prominent economic and political analysts in the US and Western Europe. To my surprise, they all reached the same conclusion, namely, that Egypt's income today is derived from five sources (all unrelated to the 'art of work'): remittances from Egyptians working abroad; oil revenues; revenues from the Suez Canal; tourism; and cotton production. Except for cotton, there is virtually no added value on these income sources. The work performed by Egyptians abroad does not count, being part of the production process of one or more of those countries; and regarding oil, the Suez Canal and tourism, your work is only a marginal source of the revenue they generate.

His words only served to reinforce my conviction that the socialist-style economic and political systems applied in many Third World countries, such as Egypt, Algeria, Libya, Cuba, Tanzania and parts of Southeast Asia and Africa, are wholly to blame for the demise of the work ethic and, with it, the spirit of enterprise and diligence. The disappearance of individual initiative and creativity motivated by personal profit and advantage, the abolition of differences among members of society engendered by the rigid socialist interpretation of 'equality', and the absence of the necessary element of risk – all of which are the result of labour laws which stifle competition and drive, and make the task of management in the private and public sectors well-nigh impossible by disallowing incentives – have created in countries following the 'socialist path to development' wide sectors of citizens unqualified for, incapable of, and unwilling to work. With every passing generation, the 'art of work' diminishes, although it is the secret of progress and welfare, and the key to stability. One of the worst disasters that can befall a people applying a socialist political and economic model (particularly those of a poor educational and cultural standard, which can be said for most of the Third World) is the development of a 'civil servant' mentality, and the erosion of the 'entrepreneurial' spirit. This permeates all levels of employees, and may extend to include the managers of public companies and politicians, up to the highest echelons. In all honesty, out of over thirty ministers in the present cabinet, I can think of only one or two who have well-developed political and social senses.

One needs to look no further for proof of this argument than to the Egyptian public sector in which, since the 1960s, the state has sunk the phenomenal sum of over 1,000 billion pounds (and yielded less than 1 per cent as an annual return on capital employed). The public sector is plunged into a state of apathy that has rendered it incapable of responding to Egypt's call for help. The situation is all the more painful if we realize that, in the normal course of events, this sector should have been able to provide Egypt annually with not less than three times the volume of US aid to the country, and Egypt must try to do without as an essential first step towards extricating itself from its sorry predicament. Egypt's heavy reliance on US aid is the inevitable result of injudicious economic and political practices over the years and by successive governments. While the present regime may not be accountable for reaching this situation, it should accept responsibility for finding a radical and speedy solution. The tables must be turned. After years in which the public was encouraged to substitute 'work' with debate and empty slogans ('Ensuring the avail-ability of goods … ', 'Raising the level of production … ', etc.), it is time to reclaim the art of work.

Egypt is not even self-sufficient in cement! Worse still: the sum spent by Egypt every day to buy the cement required for its construc-tion industry is equal to its net daily income from the Suez Canal.

How could successive governments have failed to solve the agricul-tural problem in Egypt, when its solution entails nothing more than repealing the laws which produced the present disastrous situation in the first place? In addition, despite a wide consensus on the need to allow supply and demand laws to govern landlord–tenant relations, the housing sector is bogged down by laws which continue to ensure a flood of demand and scant supply.

How can one hope to speak of 'work' and 'production' when the vast majority of public sector managers prove their failure and multiply their losses every day?

The difference between Egypt and countries such as Turkey and Greece, whose economies are steadily growing, is spelled out in Egypt's lack of productivity, effectiveness, creativity – and the simple work ethic.

It is the supreme duty of the government, and in particular the president, as the nation's chief executive, to break the vicious circle of failure that has been exacerbated over the last thirty years. It is within that vicious circle that Egyptians mislaid the 'art of work'. This is what all loyal citizens expect from their government, rather than economic policies reducing expenditures in some areas and levying heavier taxes in others. These measures fall under the heading of 'non-work'. They ask a poor man with only a few pounds to his name to redistribute that sum in his pockets, thereby increasing his poverty since he cannot increase his wealth, cash supply or value in any way – except through efficient, productive, and creative work.

3. Quality

As to the notion of quality in Egypt today, it is practically non-existent. No one can argue with the fact that standards have dropped alarmingly in this country over the last half-century. The only explanation is that it is no longer people of distinction who stand at the top of the societal pyramid, but mediocre elements intent on keeping those who can expose their mediocrity as far away as possible from any position of influence. To that end, they work actively to downgrade the notion of quality, a notion that is completely alien to them. The spread of the values, culture and standards of the mediocre elements now holding leading positions in this country makes the words of Psalm 12 come to life before our eyes every day: 'The wicked walk on every side when the violent men are exalted.'

In the light of these indicators, and of hundreds of other indicators for which there is no room to cite here, it is manifestly clear that Egyptians need to take a critical look at their poor performance, and ask themselves why the flow of foreign investments remains so modest. It is equally clear that there is no one to blame but themselves, especially since they reject any outside interference in their internal affairs. Thus, they alone are responsible not only for economic reform, but also for their economic problems.

4. A Prescription for Egypt's Economic Reform

A. *Egypt's Experiment with Economic Reform.* Let us try to assess where Egypt's experiment with monetary and economic reform stands in relation to this build-up. Certain developments are worth noting here.

Since the early 1990s, tremendous progress has been achieved in Egypt in the field of monetary reform. Many of the targeted objectives have been reached and, in general, things are moving in the right direction. The same period witnessed concerted efforts in the direction of economic reform, but much remains to be done. Of particular importance in this respect is the need for a reassessment of the role of the state in economic life: the state necessarily plays a role when it comes to vision and policies, but should be far less assertive in most areas of economic activity. Equally important is the need to dismantle the grossly inflated and ponderous Egyptian bureaucracy that continues to choke most government departments, and is a major disincentive for international investments and capital to flow into Egypt in the required volume.

It has become imperative to focus on three priorities in the area of economic reform:

1. Aspects of modern management systems, including the selection of executive leaders.
2. Human resources, training and the transfer of technology and skills.
3. The marketing sciences and the executive leaders in those areas, without whom all the efforts in the industrial and services sectors would be wasted.

This important reorientation entails a transition from the stage of the academic economists (the planners) to that of the modern management executives, for they are the ones who will turn all the great efforts at monetary and economic reform into concrete results – that is, increased production – in both the manufacturing and services sector.

B. Some Tools

1. Resources. Moving now to the economic front, Egypt is faced with a curious situation in which two divergent economic systems are coexisting in an uneasy alliance. On the one hand, there is an entrenched economic system whose cornerstones are rooted in socialism: public sector; limited agricultural holdings; state interference in all aspects of production; labour relations governed by socialist legislations; compulsory delivery of agricultural output to the state, etc; on the other, there are economic systems of a capitalist nature trying to establish themselves in a hostile environment. Obviously this attempt to accommodate two irreconcilable and, indeed, mutually exclusive economic systems is doomed to failure, and the sooner this is faced up to the better. None of the makeshift repair operations launched by successive Egyptian governments, particularly over the last few years, can succeed unless it is candidly acknowledged that the real reason for Egypt's economic decline lies in the socialist economic options to which it has subscribed for too long. Blaming Egypt's economic woes on a shortage of financial resources is a feeble excuse that all the opposition parties should reject. The shortage of financial resources is the inevitable result of specific political and economic options. The opposition should point out to the government that the latter's main function is to generate resources, or at least to create the proper climate in which they can grow. At the end of the day, it is the government alone that can be held accountable for the lack of financial resources.

2. *Management*. Many are the truthful statements that people repeat without realizing their real meaning and significance. A statement one hears very often these days is that Egypt's main problem today is 'management'. Although this is absolutely true, any attempt to elicit an explanation from people who utter the statement with a great deal of assurance reveals that – more often than not – they have no clear idea what they are talking about, and that, moreover, the word management means different things to different people.

Nevertheless, even if they are not clear on the details, they are right in their diagnosis: the main problem in Egyptians' lives in general and in their economic life in particular, is that the methods and techniques of modern management sciences and modern marketing sciences are virtually absent from government departments, the public sector, the private sector, and all the service sectors.

I have no doubt whatsoever that the Eastern bloc, made up of the Soviet Union and its legion of followers, collapsed at the end of the 1980s because of the absence of effective management in all the sectors of the socialist world, particularly in the economic sector where the absence of management led to a state of bankruptcy which brought the whole temple of socialism to crash down.

If the collapse of the Eastern bloc can be blamed in large part on poor economic management, much of the credit for the flourishing economies of the Western world and the Asian Tigers, which led to the growth of a prosperous and dynamic middle class, can be attributed to the application of modern and efficient management and marketing systems. It is worth noting in this connection that efficient management is capable not only of steering a country on the path of economic prosperity and allowing it to reap the positive social benefits that accrue, but also of dealing with crises and reversals. It was thanks only to sound management that the countries of Southeast Asia, and Mexico before them, succeeded in overcoming their financial crises in a record time, confounding the expectations of some of Egypt's pundits who were patting themselves on the back for having adopted a more cautious approach. The swift recovery of the Southeast Asian and Mexican economies proves that a country with a clear vision of where it is heading, and which proceeds to implement that vision by means of a scientific methodological approach can, when exposed to a crisis situation that causes it to slip backwards on its chosen path, regain its footing as long as the methodology is still in place.

Before going any further, it might be useful here to define exactly what success means when applied to an economic venture. This entails first clearing up a certain ambiguity which arises from the absence of any distinction in the Arabic language between the two notions of administration and management, both of which are translated as *idara* in Arabic. In fact, the two notions are quite distinct in English. While administration means the set of rules governing work in the workplace, such as personnel regulations, working hours, disciplinary measures and the like, the word management denotes something altogether different. In essence, it is the mechanism by which an enterprise achieves its desired goals which are – specifically realizing given economic returns – parallel to a process of growth, by using the tools of modern marketing sciences.

Thus the economic enterprises established in countries which adopted a system of centralized planning, the so-called command economies, could impress one with their massive size, machinery, equipment and huge workforce only if one looks upon them from the perspective of administration. But however impressive these factors may be, they mean absolutely nothing from the viewpoint of modern management, where the only criterion for success is an enterprise's ability to deploy its resources, machinery and workforce efficiently in order to realize economic returns which must not be less than the interest accruing on bank deposits.

A project which does not yield a return on investment greater than the interest on bank deposits will inevitably reach a state of bankruptcy that renders it incapable of performing its economic and other functions, the most important of which is employment and the creation of new job opportunities.

The pride with which some people continue to regard the huge enterprises which once dominated Egypt's economic landscape and which, because of the absence of effective management, failed to realize economic returns greater than the interest on bank deposits, is both strange and misplaced. What they are proud of in the final analysis is the money spent rather than the returns on expenditure, which were in most cases extremely modest, and led to the failure of the entire experiment.

Societies which confuse the notion of management in the sense I have explained, and that of administration as the system of checks and balances governing the workplace, should understand that, for all its importance, administration cannot be a vehicle for economic prosperity. The only way this can be achieved is through the application of the principles, techniques and procedures of modern management and marketing sciences.

Management, like medicine or architecture, is a profession for which special skills and training are required. Like a doctor or architect, the modern manager chooses his/her career path on the basis of personal inclination and aptitude, and then undergoes an extensive course of study and training. Promotion to a higher rung on the administrative ladder does not, in and of itself, create a modern executive manager capable of leading and planning in order to achieve the desired targets in terms of profitability and growth – while at the same time giving high priority to the development of the most important element in the success of any enterprise, its human resources.

As anyone who has had the nightmarish experience of dealing with the Egyptian bureaucracy can testify, the concept of modern management is a totally alien one as far as all government departments are concerned. Unfortunately, this is equally true of the economic units of both the public and private sectors, which are run according to a bazaar mentality having nothing to do with the spirit and mechanisms of private economic institutions operated in accordance with the principles of modern management, human resources and marketing sciences. Scientists in these fields are well aware that the vast majority of private economic establishments in Egypt today are almost totally dependent on public relations rather than on management in the modern sense of the word. Operating as they do in a general climate in which public relations reign supreme, they have spared themselves the trouble of building modern institutional systems and recruiting efficient human elements capable of running them in accordance with the principles of sound management. Building such a system is a costly business and, in addition, simple minds cannot grasp its merits, especially in the context of a business culture that venerates public relations as a short cut to power and influence.

Unless Egypt creates a general climate that is conducive to the introduction of modern management practices in government departments, public sector units and the manufacturing and service establishments of the private sector, it cannot hope to attract a significant flow of direct foreign investments. Investors are wary of pouring money into an environment that does not allow them to function in accordance with the mechanisms and techniques of modern management, human resources and marketing sciences, and it is precisely the absence of those mechanisms that stands at the root of Egypt's deteriorating economic situation. True, Egypt began to address the problem ten years ago, but it needs to adopt a far more forceful approach if it is ever to transform its business environment into an investor-friendly setting governed by the principles of modern management in all spheres of life.

Until then, the slogan 'Egypt's main problem is management', without fully understanding the real significance and implications of this diagnosis, will remain nothing more than a meaningless mantra.

3. Housing. Foremost among the problems besetting Egypt today, and which successive governments have avoided coming to grips with, are those of housing and education. Unless the root causes of these problems are addressed and serious efforts made to solve them, it is not possible to look forward to a better future.

The housing problem is highly complex, not so much because its causes are hard to understand, but because the many ineffectual attempts to solve it have created such an intricate web of relationships and conflicting interests that any attempt to bring about a radical solution today is bound to create victims. In fact, the problem is closely connected with the two aspects we have been discussing: the political aspect, and the economic aspect. An analysis of the problem that does not address its root causes and historical development would fail to achieve the purpose of diagnosing the disease and prescribe the effective cure.

The onset of the disease can be traced to the early 1950s, when the government decided to interfere in the contractual relationship between landlords and tenants of housing units, ostensibly to protect tenants from exploitation by landlords. Government interference was directed at two areas: term of lease and value of rent. Until then, lease contracts for residential housing units were based on the classical legal principle of 'sovereign will', as represented essentially in the freedom of the parties to agree on the term of the lease and the rental value payable for the leased premises. However, the July 1952 revolution, or more particularly, its leader, Gamal Abdel Nasser, decided to cast the landlord in the role of exploiter, and the tenant in the role of the victim of the former's greed. Having thus assigned roles, the revolution sided with the weaker party – that is, the tenant – whom it decided to release from any commitment as to the agreed term or value of the lease. Obviously the revolution did not look at the issue from an economic point of view, in the sense that it did not take into account the long-term effects of these measures on the construction market, the housing market, urban planning, etc. Rather, it saw it in political, not to say demagogical terms, as borne out by the fact that the regime sought to make as much political capital as possible by having the president himself announce the freezing of rents and all subsequent reductions thereof. It is irrelevant here to discuss the real motives of the revolution and its leader in this matter. I am even willing to concede that they were well-intentioned, and that their desire to protect 'the weak' was sincere. All this is water under bridge. Today, the experience must be judged in terms of results, not intentions.

What are the results Egyptians are reaping today from this misguided policy? The revolution wished to protect the tenant from the landlord – did it actually succeed in doing so? Did it achieve its purpose of making homes available at prices accessible to ordinary people of the middle and working classes, and to small farmers and peasants? In fact, a direct result of its decision to release the tenant from his obligation to observe the term of the lease or the rental value agreed upon has been to discourage investment in the area of housing, as prospective investors realized that they could derive higher returns from trade or even from interest accruing on bank deposits, than from building and letting housing units. All aspects of the problem stem from that fact. In the context of restrictive legislations, investors were left with one of two options: either to steer clear of the housing market – and the enormous discrepancy between supply and demand in this area attests to the predominance of this option – or to build housing units for sale or rent in exchange for large sums of money paid under the counter as key money or non-refundable 'advance rent'. Thus the three major problems in the housing sector (a severe shortage of supply as compared to the ever increasing demand for units for rent, an abundance of housing units up for sale and a dearth of those available for rent and, finally, the exorbitant sums demanded by landlords outside the contract) all result from the fact that government interference in lease contracts removed the incentive of profit which alone can induce an investor to move into a given area of investment. They also rendered the construction of housing units for rent a losing proposition, yielding a return far below that accruing as interest on money placed in the bank, not to mention the problems of dealing with tenants, whom the new housing laws considered to be victims of greedy and exploitive landlords. To go back to the question: did the housing legislations introduced by the revolution succeed in protecting tenants?

There was a time, before the revolution, when an Egyptian citizen could always find a home for a reasonable rent within their means. Today, they waste years of their life looking for a home, having already spent years saving up for the price or the key money to be paid to the owner, the only one to profit from the new formula. Who then is the ultimate beneficiary? Can the 1952 revolution claim to have achieved its objective of providing reasonably-priced housing for the people? Or would it not be fair to say that tenants are the main, indeed, the only, casualties of a misguided housing policy?

So complex has the issue become, so far-reaching its ramifications that, although I am in absolutely no doubt that the disastrous housing situation is the direct result of a blithe disregard of free-market laws, I cannot condone a solution based on deregulating rents and allowing landlords to fix them at their sole discretion. Such a solution would deal a death-blow to the millions of Egyptians whose incomes are not market-compatible: scraping by on their government salaries or pensions, they can certainly not afford free-market prices. No self-respecting regime could ever take such a step.

The only viable solution is to deal separately with two categories of existing housing units: firstly, old buildings used for residential purposes, and secondly, old buildings put to commercial use and newly-built units – whether put to residential or commercial use. In respect of the first category of old units inhabited by individuals or families, rents could be raised by no more than 5 to 10 per cent, a rate of increase that could definitely be met by the salaried class while giving landlords, usually belonging to the same class, a slightly better income that may encourage them to undertake some minor repair and maintenance works to prevent the dilapidation of old buildings that the Egyptian people are witnessing.

As for leased premises that are put to commercial use, such as doctors' clinics, lawyers' offices, offices for financial or trading activities and shops, a new system should be devised to double their rent annually. It is absurd to pay a niggardly rent for premises that are put to commercial use, and which bring in thousands of pounds every day. It is equally absurd to consider the landlord here to be the exploiting party and the tenant his victim. The rents payable in new buildings should be left entirely to the laws of the free market, with no interference whatsoever from the state to impose indefinite lease contracts or set up committees to determine the rent, which should be exclusively subject to the laws of supply and demand. This is the only way out of the housing tragedy that successive governments have failed to resolve effectively, because they disregarded the true causes and could not, for political reasons, face the painful fact that the government itself had sown the seeds of the housing tragedy in the 1950s.

4. Education. If the problem of housing casts a long shadow that promises to stretch well into the future, so too does that of education. There can be no hope of a better life for the coming generations of Egyptians, unless serious attempts are made today to find a radical solution to this problem. Any such attempts must depart not from doctrinaire political givens, but from an in-depth analysis of the crisis and its causes. Like the housing problem, the problem of education needs to be carefully diagnosed so that it may be effectively treated.

The picture was not always so bleak – in fact, quite the contrary. In the 1920s and 1930s, Egyptian education enjoyed its golden age, thanks to a generation of outstanding Egyptians who were pioneers in their respective fields, such as Dr Mesharrafa in mathematics,[2] Dr Hussein Fawzy in the sciences,[3] Dr Aly Ibrahim,[4] Dr Mahmoud Mahfouz[5] and others in medicine, and scores of illustrious names in literature and law, as well as many others in all areas of scholarly achievement, all of whom benefited from the best that Western education had to offer.

We might well ask what has befallen education in Egypt since, and why it has sunk to its present regrettable level. The answer is that education at all levels received a crippling blow when it became subservient to the orientations of Egypt's new rulers following the success of the 1952 revolution. The seeds of the tragedy were sown when the victorious revolution placed an officer at the head of education in the country, a military man with no experience in this area, and whose own educational and cultural background was very modest.[6] The reference for the reader interested in that particular detail is the study published by Dr Anwar Abdel Malek, research master at the CNRS, Paris, under the title *L'Egypte, Société Militaire,*[7] in which he analyses the educational and cultural background of the revolutionary council in general, and of the man fully entrusted with the supervision of education in Egypt in particular.

It is from the moment education was placed in the hands of someone who knew nothing of education or culture, from the moment politics became the prime mover of all educational policies and programmes, that education in Egypt began its downward slide. Once at a peak level that it had attained thanks to outstanding Egyptian pioneers in different branches of knowledge, education has dropped into an abyss of backwardness, thanks to those who should never have been entrusted with its fate in the first place; nor did the crippling blow strike secular education alone. It also affected the ancient centre of religious learning, Al-Azhar University, subjecting it to political currents and placing it in the hands of men whose mastery of Arabic and of Islamic culture was far inferior to the level of the original Azhar primary school certificate.

The great man of letters, Dr Taha Hussein, left us with a profound and accurate study, *The Future of Culture in Egypt*, in two volumes of 550 pages, which he wrote in 1938.[8] Today, the extent of the tragedy which has befallen Egyptian education is such that to try and diagnose it, let alone to propose a remedy, would require many more volumes. All I hope to achieve with the present study is to show that a problem of this magnitude cannot be solved by the haphazard and stopgap solutions with which the present government is experimenting, and which have led nowhere.

The problem of education in Egypt today is closely linked to the basic production process: as long as no radical solution has been found for the agricultural problem, and as long as the state continues to play its present patriarchal role in the areas of economics and industry and to pursue its current employment policy, Egyptians will continue to struggle through years of learning, from school to university, only to end up as government employees and petty clerks. The government seems incapable of instituting radical reforms, either because it lacks vision, or because it adopts a politically biased – often demagogical – view of all matters. No doubt it is this which prevents the government from putting an end to free education for all, from limiting the number of students entering universities, from expanding in the area of technical education, from allowing private universities to be set up and from refraining from imposing its own views on institutions of learning.

In spite of all that has been said, the connection which exists between the crisis of education in Egypt and the long absence of democracy from Egyptian lives should not be overlooked. A climate of freedom and democracy encourages the growth of culture and intellectual creativity, and allows the development of a better and healthier educational system. Conversely, in a climate of totalitarianism, culture and intellectual creativity wither and fade, and a backward educational system, subservient to the whims of the regime, imposes itself. In a situation of this kind, we come across such inexplicable phenomena as the political decision to stop the teaching of French in Egyptian schools, in retaliation for France's participation in the tripartite aggression of 1956. This example graphically illustrates how education can suffer when it is used as a political tool by people who epitomize ignorance and backwardness.

Of paramount importance at this juncture is that the people of Egypt should realize that policies can be judged only by their results, not by the intentions behind them. A ruler is like the captain of a ship who is expected to carry his passengers safely from shore to shore. He is responsible for calculating the speed and direction of winds and waves; he cannot claim that unexpected winds or waves caught him by surprise, because a ship's captain, by definition, is supposed to know such things. One must not accept excuses about unexpected circumstances and events from the people in charge, whatever their position is. It is precisely to optimize results in unfavourable circumstances that they were placed in positions of responsibility in the first place. If one applies such a criterion in judging policies, one can also judge the success or failure of public figures. In countries where democracy and public freedoms prevail, public figures are judged on the basis of the results they achieve, not of their intentions. Established democracies do not differentiate between good and bad excuses when judging the failure of public figures to do their duty. A case in point is the 1968 crisis in Paris, responsibility for which was laid at the door of no less revered a personage than President Charles de Gaulle.[9] This example should serve as a lesson to us all.

I have referred in some of my writings to what I call the 'engineered reform phase', which is a stage of planned reform. Egypt has embarked on this stage, but so far the steps it has taken on the path of reform have been slow. Meanwhile, the problems crying out for reform are growing at a much faster pace, and the lag between the speed of reforms and the rate at which these problems are growing carries implications that are too dangerous to ignore.

Egypt must also base its economic and social options on a realistic appraisal of where things stand. In this, it should be guided by the example of the Asian countries which are now prospering thanks, in large part, to the contribution of efficient, highly-qualified people motivated by the ideals of the age: political liberalism, market economy, and modern management systems capable of compressing the time frame required for change and development.

These are just a few notes in the margin of the most important subject in Egypt today, which can be summed up in the question on everyone's lips: where is the Egyptian society heading? One can only hope that the answer is not couched in such vague, poetic formulas as 'towards a brighter future' or 'towards a dark future'. This kind of response is totally out of synch with the spirit of the age, which requires measured answers based on precise criteria. Such criteria, or benchmarks, can help a society determine whether it is on the right course, and so can a comparison with the experience of other countries in instituting reforms – specifically the path they took and the speed at which the process was accomplished.

NOTES

1. Liberalist Egyptian professor of economics at the American University in Cairo.
2. (1898–1950). Ali Mustafa Musharrafa Pasha was an Egyptian scientific researcher who added much to diverse scientific fields; he is also the author of a novel written entirely in colloquial Arabic.
3. (1900–88). Egyptian intellectual who studied medicine at the Egyptian University; after his graduation (1925), he travelled to France to study ophthalmology. However, he abandoned his medical studies for two different things: classical music and marine lives. After six years in Paris, he returned to Egypt to two different paths, a scientific research path as professor in the Faculty of Science, and a path as a scholar who profoundly advocated Western culture; in parallel, he wrote extensively about symphonic music. When Sadat signed the Camp David Treaty with Israel, Hussein Fawzi was one of the strongest supporters of Sadat's initiative in general, and to naturalization between Egypt and Israel in particular. He continued to write in favour of Western civilization until he died in 1988. Many refer to him as 'Sindbad' due to the fact that he spent three years in the Indian Ocean (in the 1930s) pursuing marine researches.
4. The first Egyptian dean of the Faculty of Medicine of Cairo University; he became Egypt's minister of health in the 1940s.
5. A key political figure in Egypt in the 1970s, 1980s, and 1990s; he became minister of health in the Sadat era.
6. Kamal Eddin Hussein, one of the members of Nasser's closed circle who was among the leaders of the coup d'état (subsequently called 'revolution') of 23 July 1952.
7. Abdel Malek, Anwar, *Égypte, société militaire* [Egypt, Military Society] (Paris: Éditions du Seuil, 1962).
8. Hussein, Taha, *Mustaqbal al thaqafa fi misr* [The Future of Culture in Egypt] (Cairo: Dar al Ma'aref, 1938). The book, although nationalist and advocating independence, also called for the adoption of certain European standards.
9. (1890–1970). French general, founder and first president of the Fifth Republic of France in 1959. In May 1968, he had to face wide protests, demonstrations and strikes, especially by young people, which questioned his legitimacy. He retired in 1969 after losing a referendum to change the French Senate into an advisory body while extending powers to regional councils.

9

Realizing Progress

1. CURING THE 'ANTI-CHANGE CULTURE'

One cannot talk of reform, even in the most perfunctory way, without referring to what I call the 'anti-change culture' pervading every aspect of the Arabs' lives. In the world of management, all training programmes for senior cadres begin by emphasizing the importance of managing change. Rapid change is a feature of modern life, and the ability to adapt to the accelerated pace of change and deal with the many variables involved is par for the course. However, Arabic-speaking societies belong to a culture that venerates the past, and sets great store by traditions and customs established through long usage. This makes for a mindset that is averse to change in general, and for any change to be perceived as a threat to their traditions in particular. They are not the only ones exhibiting this cultural peculiarity. Another Arab country launched a campaign in the early 1990s under the slogan 'Development without change!' As development is by definition a dynamic process involving a forward motion from one situation to another, to talk of development as a static process that will miraculously unfold without bringing about any change is a contradiction in terms, not to say an oxymoron. Nevertheless, the slogan is significant in that it reveals the strong resistance to change in the Arab culture, whose sociological formation is still dominated by the notions of tribalism and kinship, not of modern citizenship.

Sceptics who warn against the dangers of rapid change do have a point. However, the time for abstract reflections is fast running out. Any society whose problems continue to grow at a faster rate than it can come up with the proper remedies is doomed to sink into a downward spiral. By the same token, if treatment proceeds at a faster rate than the growth of problems, the situation is bound to improve.

Yet before the values of progress can take root in any society, the general cultural, intellectual, educational and information climate in that society must be such as to allow them to spread and flourish; more specifically, it must be a climate that is not resistant to change. A look at the most dramatic models of progress in the last fifty years shows that they were the result of successful experiments in management reform before being the result of experiments in economic reform. And management reform, like all modern management sciences, can only come about in a general climate that is receptive to change. Creative interaction with and feedback from change is at the heart of successful management, and that is why business administration courses in the top universities worldwide consider 'managing change' to be the core element of successful management.

Many in the Arab societies may be unable, through no fault of their own, to grasp the point made here, although it is an elementary principle of modern management sciences. All training and study programmes for senior management executives in the developed world proceed from a number of basic premises.

The propensity of certain cultures, especially in ancient societies, to cling to the status quo and oppose change is understandable from the historical and sociological points of view. But these cultures are, by definition, inimical to progress, and their shortcomings must be revealed to those who aspire to development and success. A culture that embraces change and is willing to interact with it positively and constructively is primed for progress and success.

Modern management adopts a pragmatic, non-dogmatic approach to change that tries, as far as possible, to be devoid of ideology.

The guiding principle of modern management techniques, which have steered the West and the countries of East Asia to their present level of progress, is 'constant and purposeful interaction with change'.

In my opinion, the main enemy of a culture of change is the ideological approach. Modern management techniques are based on mechanisms which have proved successful in practice and which were not adopted for ideological considerations. In fact, ideology itself is subject to this law, in the sense that while the problem-solving approach of ideologues proceeds from a theoretical/intellectual premise, management leaders adopt an empirical/pragmatic approach.

If progress is a function of successful management, and if a prerequisite of successful management is the spread of the values of progress, it follows that a general climate which accepts the critical mind and is willing to coexist in a constructive manner with change is a cornerstone of progress.

2. THE MAKING OF THE FUTURE

Proceeding as it does from so-called constants while ignoring the givens of contemporary reality, this closed system feeds the propensity for dealing with challenges in a static, fatalistic manner. Such a passive approach is natural in cultures which believe the future is a kind of mythical being that already exists in its final shape, regardless of anything they do today. A very different approach is found in societies whose citizens in general, and whose elites in particular, believe they can play an effective role in shaping the future. These societies do not believe in an abstract, absolute being called 'the Future'; rather, they believe, as the famous exponent of existentialism Jean-Paul Sartre put it, that 'there is no such thing called the future; the future is what we make today'. The absence of effective participation encourages a deterministic perception of the future as preordained and inevitable, which in turn encourages the belief that this mythical being is shaped by others to serve their own interests. From there, it is one easy step to subscribe wholeheartedly to the conspiracy theory!

It is true that the history of humanity, of life itself, is one of bloody conflict and ferocious struggle. But it is also true that the engine of history is driven by people who believe that their actions can affect the course of events, people who see themselves as active participants in shaping the future, not by those who sit on the sidelines and wait passively for whatever life decides to throw at them. The former strive to create a future whose features conform as closely as possible to their ideal vision of what that future should be; the latter wait for a future that can only be disappointing because it is the creation of others. The tendency to believe that no human agency can affect the shape of things to come is natural in those such as Arab-speaking societies, where destiny, not human will, is seen as playing the leading role in determining the present and the future. This feature is more salient in the Arab culture than it is in any other. Of course, every culture believes in destiny to one degree or another. The real issue is the hold that belief has over the lives of the majority of people within a society. In some societies, people sit and wait passively for whatever fate has in store for them, on the grounds that they can do nothing to change what is written in the stars. In others, people believe they have a say in determining their lot, on the grounds that the future is still in the making and what they do in the present can affect its ultimate shape.

I wrote this part after rereading two books I had first read over thirty years ago, when I was in my early 20s. One, entitled *The Incoherence of the Philosophers*, is by Abu Hamid Al-Ghazali, known as Algazel in mediaeval Europe;[1] the other, entitled *The Incoherence* of *the Incoherence*, is by Ibn Rushd, or Averroes as he is known in the West,[2] the most outstanding Arab philosopher of his time. The books represent a bitter conflict between the representatives of two schools: Al-Ghazali was the proponent of tradition and orthodoxy, Ibn Rushd believed in the primacy of reason. The conflict waged ten centuries ago ended in the victory of the former over the latter, with disastrous consequences for the Arabic-speaking societies today. That is why Arabs have become spectators rather than participants on the stage of life, looking on as others act in the drama unfolding before their eyes. Like all audiences, their role is limited to applauding or booing the actors or, occasionally, to adding new jokes to their already impressive repertoire.

While Arabs turned their backs on Ibn Rushd, Western Europe adopted his defence of Aristotelian philosophy at a time when Europe was the arena for a similar conflict between reason and tradition. But while the school of reason prevailed in Europe, Arabs followed the teachings of Al-Ghazali, elevating him to the rank of Hujjat al-Islam (proof of Islam). In fact, the man who deserved that title was Ibn Rushd, whose enlightened approach shines through in one of his most famous works, *Fasl al-maqal*, in which he calls philosophy the companion and foster-sister of the Shari'a.[3]

3. INTRODUCING MODERN MANAGEMENT TECHNIQUES

The fatalistic approach of Arab society to the future is even more at odds with the times if viewed from the perspective of modern management, the newest member of the group of social sciences and, since its introduction as an independent discipline in the second half of the twentieth century, arguably the most important one of all. The word 'impossible' does not exist in the lexicon of modern management science, which assumes that, as long as one has a vision of one's future goal, as long as one lays down the strategies, plans, programmes and policies that will serve as one's bridge towards that future and, finally, as long as one makes optimal use of available resources – particularly human resources – one is sure to reach one's goal. But such an outlook needs a cultural climate that is not dominated by a fatalistic acceptance of the vicissitudes of fortune, a climate in which people recognize that the shape of their future will be determined largely by their actions in the here and now. It also requires a climate in which citizens are encouraged to participate actively in all spheres of life, as well as one in which a healthy process of social mobility allows the best elements in society, the men and women who are equipped to help it achieve its desired goals, to rise to the top of the societal pyramid.

4. ENABLING WOMEN

How such a climate can be achieved is a subject beyond the limitations of one chapter or even an entire book. In writing this chapter, I was hoping only to draw attention to the magnitude and complexity of the problem Arabic-speaking societies are facing. The question of society's ability to shed its fatalistic attitude in favour of a more affirmative approach as a precondition for rising to the challenges of the present and the future is related to many other issues, such as people's understanding of religion and the prevailing religious culture, the cultural formation of religious leaders, educational programmes and curricula, general freedoms, and the degree to which democratic values have taken root in society. It is also related to the general cultural climate as well as to one of the most important issues in any society, namely the status of women. As a general rule, civic participation in societies which marginalize the role of half their citizens tends to be poor. In fact, I believe the status of women in any society is a pivotal issue in its cultural formation and intellectual development. Until Arabs reach a stage in which the notion of complete equality between the sexes takes hold in society, and until the necessary mechanisms to translate that notion into practical measures are put in place, they are doomed to remain hostage to their fatalistic mindset, allowing destiny to rule their lives while they sit on the sidelines waiting for whatever tomorrow may bring instead of playing an active role in shaping the future.

5. PROMOTING POSITIVITY

The reader is entitled to ask what the common denominator between the various issues addressed by this chapter is. The answer to that question lies in the account I gave earlier about a debate between two Egyptian intellectuals over the Nairobi agreement related to Sudan;[4] the debate encapsulates two different attitudes towards the event: one static, which proceeds from the assumption that we are helpless onlookers with no choice but to wait for the future to unfold as it will; the other dynamic, which assumes that we can, and indeed must, have a say in determining its ultimate shape. In other words, the common denominator between all the issues raised in the chapter is the Arab mindset and the passive way the Arabs deal with external challenges, present and future. Their thinking has to become more forceful, dynamic and imaginative if they are to rise to the many challenges facing them. The greater the degree of their involvement in and awareness of the realities of the age, and the more they liberate themselves from obsolete slogans, the better their prospects of confronting these challenges successfully. This applies in all cases, not only in respect of the Nairobi agreement, which is just an example used to illustrate the fundamental message of this chapter. What needs to be realized before it is too late, is that the static mindset of Arabic-speaking societies can only lead to greater loss, while a dynamic approach based on active participation can do just the opposite.

6. SHIFTING THE EDUCATIONAL SYSTEMS TOWARDS INNOVATION

Towards the end of 2000, the American University in Cairo invited me to speak on the nature of the educational reforms I wanted to see introduced in Egypt. In my lecture, which I delivered in the university's Greek Campus, I spoke extensively about the difference between a 'qualitative' change in an educational system and a 'quantitative' change. I said that the Arabic-speaking societies had paid scant attention to the former, because their educational philosophy continues to be based on rote system and memory tests rather than on promoting creativity and dialogue (as opposed to monologue). Education is not seen as an interactive process, but as a one-way street in which the teacher is a 'transmitter' of knowledge and the student a passive 'receiver' of that knowledge.

In the first quarter of 2001, I was invited by Princeton University and Columbia University on the East Coast of the US, and the University of California at Berkeley on the West Coast, to deliver a series of lectures to postgraduate students in Middle Eastern studies. In my lectures, I stressed the need for an educational revolution in the region if we want a scenario of peace (real peace based on international legitimacy and the principles of international law) and comprehensive development (economic, cultural and social) to prevail. For all its complexity, such a revolution would be based essentially on a simple philosophy of instilling in students a set of values that I call 'values of progress'.

Since August 2001, I have devoted much of my time to developing this idea further. In a way, my interest in promoting the notion of values of progress provided an outlet for the frustration I felt at the way public debate in the Arab society tends to degenerate into private squabbles. Any topic can spark off a furious controversy: Mohamed 'Ali, Taha Hussein, Gamal Abdel Nasser, Anwar Sadat, secularism, enlightenment, modernity, globalization or peace in the Middle East are equally divisive, splitting people across seemingly unbridgeable ideological chasms and entrenching them still further in their respective closed systems. The rules of rational and objective debate are spurned in favour of a dialogue of the deaf, in which the protagonists engage in mutual recriminations and insults, heaping abuse and accusations against one another.

When I began looking for a subject that would not polarize society, or would at least polarize it less sharply than most topics have, the only one that seemed to fit the bill was the notion of values of progress that I had touched upon earlier in several articles and lectures. Not a subject that can split society into opposing camps – Islamists versus non-Islamists, socialists versus capitalists – it is to a large extent non-ideological and, as such, lends itself to an objective and neutral debate that needs not descend into the usual pattern of dogmatic intransigence.

Perhaps this was wishful thinking on my part, a scenario that is closer to fantasy than to reality. But rigid patterns can only be broken by those who have the capacity to dream, and the gift of imagination. With this in mind, some schools of modern management require senior managers to exhibit two concomitant characteristics, which at first glance may seem contradictory: power of imagination on the one hand, and a sense of reality on the other. In actual fact, however, these characteristics are not mutually exclusive and are often present at one and the same time in ordinary people. It is these individuals who make successful senior managers. I hope that my dream of contemporary Egyptian intellectuals and public opinion capable of dealing with the subject of values of progress in a manner free from factionalism and preconception will see the daylight.[5] I hope it strikes the proper balance between power of imagination and a sense of reality, otherwise it will be nothing more than an exercise in escapism, a mirage to which I turned, out of a deep sense of despair at the inhospitable climate for any reasoned and objective debate in the Arabic-speaking societies today, where name-calling and stone-throwing have replaced logical argumentation.

In 1784, the great philosopher Immanuel Kant published a remarkable essay under the title 'An Answer to the Question: "What is Enlightenment?" ' What he had to say on the subject is worthy of contemplation in the current situation of the Arab societies:

A revolution may well put an end to autocratic despotism and to rapacious or power-seeking oppression, but it will never produce a true reform in ways of thinking. Instead, new prejudices, like the ones they replaced, will serve as a leash to control the great unthinking mass ... For enlightenment of this kind, all that is needed is freedom. And the freedom in question is the most innocuous form of all freedoms to make public use of one's reason in all matters.

Kant believed that enlightenment came from using the human mind, not the human instincts, not the human links with the past, and not the human emotions. That, I think, sums up the message that this chapter has tried to convey.

FINDING SOLUTIONS FOR EGYPT AS AN EXAMPLE OF THE ARABIC-SPEAKING SOCIETIES

It is common in Egypt today to hear people from different walks of life bemoaning the 'death' of ethics, the erosion of the country's moral fibre and the proliferation of many ignoble values, such as envy. Unfortunately, they are right. But it is necessary to question why this state of affairs has come about. I believe the collapse of moral principles and the spread of envy, not only between people but also between classes, can be traced to a specific mechanism. The previous chapters attempted to trace and analyse the root causes of the 'Egyptian problem' as I see it. Now I shall explore the solutions available in light of that analysis.

So – what is to be done? Today Egypt finds itself facing one of the most propitious moments for making a choice in its contemporary history. Indeed, with the exception of just such a moment following the success of the 1952 revolution, proffering a chance the ruling regime failed to seize, the present juncture is the best opportunity Egypt has had in recent times for making a choice. Yet, like all choices, this one is loaded with implications.

The difficulty with choice as a philosophical concept lies in its very nature, suggesting as it does a decision to take one of several paths. But recognizing the difficulty inherent in making the choice does not negate the existence of a great historical opportunity for Egypt to choose among the available options. If it so wishes, and provided its decision-makers are up to the task, Egypt can rid itself of economic dependence and, consequently, of the two forms of political dependence it has known under Nasser and Sadat. It can harness huge potential and creative powers capable of generating tremendous sources of revenue for its people from agriculture, industry, tourism, mining and oil resources, in addition to tripling, or even quadrupling, its present income from the remittances of its nationals working abroad. It can streamline the bloated and ruinous bureaucracy engendered by a totalitarian regime and by the absence of freedom and democracy. It can put an end to its tragic and draining involvement in problems outside its own territories, problems which the parties concerned are in no hurry to solve as long as they can continue to feed on the tragedy, and make political capital from the wounds of their people.

There is no doubt that the Egyptian public, having learned its lesson from bitter experience, tends not to support Egypt's involvement in such problems. But it is not enough to avoid becoming embroiled in external problems. Egypt should also avoid becoming further entangled in an economic system that has proved to be a total failure, and which has led the country to the brink of bankruptcy; a system that has rendered Egypt unable to feed its people without crippling loans which make a mockery of any talk of political and economic independence.

The situation calls for action on two fronts, political and economic, the latter being a function of the former and not the other way round, as Marxists and others – notably military juntas – would have one believe.

IMPERATIVE NEED FOR REMOVAL OF THE IMPEDIMENTS ON PROGRESS

Today I stand on a halfway point between optimism and its opposite, when it comes to the question of whether the Egyptians can, over the short and medium term, rid their society of some of the main cultural ills impeding its progress, such as:

1. The 'big talk' syndrome.
2. The tendency to sing one's own praises.
3. The exaltation of a glorious past that exists only in the imagination.
4. A culture of people, not institutions.
5. A lack of objectivity and the growth of individualism.
6. A feeling of superiority over others because of religion.
7. No belief in the universality of science and knowledge.
8. A narrow margin of tolerance.
9. No acceptance of the 'Other'.
10. A tendency to live in the past and show little interest in the future.

11. The spread of a male chauvinist mentality that does not accord equal rights to women, with the result that society runs on half steam, with fully one half of its potential lying idle. As to the other half, the male supremacists, they are maladjusted personalities suffering from feelings of inadequacy, for which they compensate by asserting their innate superiority on the basis of gender. A society that relegates half its citizens to a lower status than the other half cannot hope to build a good present or achieve a better future.

Although I am of two minds when it comes to assessing ability of Egypt's society to rid itself of these serious defects that are stunting its growth and paralyzing its effectiveness, one recent development makes me more inclined to optimism than pessimism. I am talking about the generation of under-thirties who are taking a great interest in Egypt's reality and future and far less interest in the affairs of others. This is a major achievement, albeit one that is not due to any internal factor but to the information revolution, computers and the Internet which have put this generation in touch with the world and allowed it to rearrange its priorities in their rightful order.

1. Reform of Parliamentary Elections

A necessary first step towards solving the problems now besetting the Egyptian body politic is to abolish the present system of parliamentary elections, and replace it with one that would serve the goal of freedom and democracy to which the majority of Egyptians aspire. Such a step would be difficult in the present circumstances without a positive initiative from the presidency, led by the president of the republic himself. Until that hope materializes, all the forces of freedom and democracy should champion one of the noblest of national causes: electing their leaders. All the millions of eligible voters should register and go to the polls at all kinds of elections.

This would allow a wise and moderate opposition to increase its seats in parliament, a natural development expected and, indeed, favoured by President Mubarak. That much can be understood from the many speeches in which he has reiterated his faith in the gradual and constant growth of democracy in Egypt, a growth without sudden starts and leaps which may cause imbalance and confusion in Egyptian society. While there is no disputing the validity of this view, it is important to differentiate between the time frame in which the opposition would like to see this process unfold, and that contemplated by the government. The ideal probably lies somewhere in between.

2. Abolition of Totalitarian Regime Mechanisms

Reform also entails the abolition of such mechanisms as the 'administrative control agency', which were introduced under the totalitarian regime. These mechanisms cannot coexist with the Office of the Public Prosecutor (the only mechanism which in a democracy enjoys jurisdiction over matters under the purview of those extrajudicial bodies invented by a totalitarian system) in a political system based on legality, on the separation of powers and on the sanctity of the judiciary as a power equal to the legislative and the executive. We call upon the presidency to set up a committee of the best minds in Egypt (including those who are opponents of the regime) to explain to the president that all such bodies operating independently from the Office of the Public Prosecutor make a mockery of the principle of an independent judiciary, the backbone of freedom and the rule of law. How can anyone imagine that employees of a body such as the Administrative Control Agency, none of whom belongs to the judiciary, can accomplish what the Office of the Public Prosecutor is supposedly incapable of doing, although the latter is responsible for representing society as a prosecuting power in all matters involving criminal acts against the rights of individuals or society? And how can anyone understand why the office of the Socialist Public Prosecutor – a title totally devoid of any meaning – is not merged in the Office of the Public Prosecutor? Finally, a text should be introduced to the by-laws of the People's Assembly, barring access to the chairmanship of that venerable body to anyone who has not been elected by the people as a member of the Assembly. The selection of the Speaker of the People's Assembly must be made by the assembly itself and not, as was the case in 1957–84, by the executive.

3. Moving Towards Different Types of Minister

Egypt should also move away from the pattern of technocratic ministers to that of political ones, bearing in mind that ministers in democratic countries are always political figures, not technicians, while in totalitarian countries the opposite holds true. The explanation for this phenomenon lies in the fact that, in countries under a totalitarian system of government, a minister is merely a senior civil servant entrusted with the technical management of his/her ministry, while in democracies a minister is a political figure placed at the head of a ministry to make sure that the strategy of the government/party is implemented in that ministry's area of competence – a strategy which, more often than not, that very same minister helped formulate. In Eastern bloc countries – headed by the Soviet Union – ministries are teeming with technicians, particularly engineers, whereas in the democratic world, ministers are prominent political figures in the ruling party. It is not unusual in those countries for the minister of health, for example, to be drawn from outside the medical profession; however, he/she will be fully cognizant of and committed to his/her party's medical policy, and will deploy all the resources of his/her ministry to serve the party line in this respect. Similarly, the ministers of industry, power or agriculture will not be former civil servants in those ministries as is the case in totalitarian regimes.

For Egypt to break out of the mould of technocratic or merchandise ministers in which it is presently mired is easier said than done, however. The totalitarian regime, which lasted close on thirty years in Egypt, naturally destroyed the conditions favourable to the emergence of political figures who can only be discovered and groomed in a political climate based on a multiparty rather than a one-party system. But despite the bleakness of the present picture, which led the late political writer Ihsan Abdel Quddus[6] to describe the ministerial changes of 16 July 1984 as 'managerial changes', Egypt remains a huge reservoir of untapped political talents. The presidency should make every effort to seek them out; neither through its security apparatus, in which the Egyptian people have lost all faith; nor through the civil service hierarchy; but by casting a global and penetrating look at Egypt's public figures who have long been kept away from the channels of higher executive authority by the wall of totalitarianism. It is depressing to see the kind of ministers hatched by the totalitarian regime. In spite of the great strides towards democracy in recent years, the vast majority of ministers who have held office over the past thirty years do not seem to be intellectually or culturally above the level of a high-school graduate in a country with a flourishing cultural life, such as France, for example.

4. Readjustment of the National Democratic Party

There is also an urgent need for the ruling National Democratic Party to change the form and scope of its sphere of influence, which now resembles that of the Socialist Union when it was the only party in the political arena. The current situation not only weakens the legal opposition parties but also, and to an equal degree, the NDP itself. Moreover, it expands the sphere of influence of underground political movements skilled at coming up with catchy slogans but not with specific programmes. And, at the end of the day, it is the commitment to a political programme that distinguishes a party from a movement.

5. Detachment from a Glorified Past

Another tendency the political leadership should rid itself of is that of glorifying Egypt's history, presumably to instil a sense of pride and to make the dismal reality in which most Egyptians are living more palatable. Rather than feeling that their 5,000-year history (President Sadat repeated '7,000' so often that he nearly convinced everyone it was true!) places Egypt above all other nations, they should feel guilty that they have frittered away the glorious legacy of their ancestors. A history such as theirs qualifies them for a flourishing present and a promising future. Instead, where their ancestors built beautiful edifices that are still standing after fifty centuries, they build flimsy edifices that crumble into dust after only a few years, not to say months. A nation which gave birth in one single generation to such men of genius as Ahmed Shawki,[7] Hafez Ibrahim,[8] Taha Hussein,[9] Abbas El Aqqad,[10] Tewfik El Hakim,[11] El Manfalouty,[12] Mustapha Sadeq El Rafei,[13] Abdel Rahman El Rafei,[14] Mustapha Mesharrafa,[15] El Sanhuri,[16] Sa'd Zaghloul,[17] Abdel Khaleq Sarwat,[18] Mahmoud Said,[19] Mokhtar,[20] Sayed Darwish,[21] Mohamed Abdel Wahhab,[22] Ahmed Amin,[23] Zaki Mubarak,[24] El Mazny[25] and scores of others, should wonder why it is so barren today, and make every effort to get out of the cycle of mediocrity in which it is caught.

6. Abandonment of Misleading Vocabulary

Among the most pressing tasks of the political leadership in a situation such as the one prevailing in Egypt today is to stop misleading the public with honeyed words and rosy dreams that have no basis in reality. Unfortunately, the two late presidents, Nasser and Sadat, consistently misled the public with glowing accounts of a present that existed only in the realm of the imagination, and a future that had more to do with wishful thinking than with hard facts. One can hardly forget President Nasser's description of an army which suffered one of the worst defeats in military history as 'the strongest deterrent force in the Middle East', or his euphoric references to the missiles Al Qaher and Al Zafer (the Conqueror and the Victorious),[26] and to the Egyptian industry which, he claimed, could now 'manufacture everything' from 'a needle to a missile'. Nor can anyone forget President Sadat's designation of 1980 as 'the year of plenty', when 'every Egyptian would have a home with a large living-room' overlooking a 'beautiful view'! Equally memorable are his sanguine references to Egypt as a 'State of institutions' where 'the reign of democracy holds sway' and 'the sovereignty of the law' is paramount. He went so far as to claim that Egypt had surpassed Britain in establishing the foundations of democracy, noting that the British monarch could order the dissolution of parliament while he could not do so without a public referendum! As the aim here is not to vilify anyone or to apportion blame, but rather to draw lessons from the errors of the recent past, these few examples of how the political leadership misled the public will be sufficient.

It can be said, of course, that honeyed words have not been a hallmark of President Mubarak's regime, which does not go in for falsely reassuring accounts of Egypt's present reality or for extravagant promises of a rosy future. However, if it is true that for the past few years the political leadership has displayed a commendable degree of realism and restraint in addressing the public, it is also true that the government in Egypt adopts a defensive posture in the face of any criticism, as though all were well in the best of all possible worlds. If any fair-minded observer must admit that official statements in recent years have been free of empty promises, he/she cannot have failed to notice that they are often made up of a curious blend of facts and hopes. This is particularly evident in the flood of official statements about the high quality of Egyptian goods, and about the level of local expertise and know-how being up to the highest international standards. While such positive talk can inspire a spirit of national pride and determination among the masses – which can spur them on to improve performance and increase production – one must not lose sight of the dangers inherent in promoting an attitude of complacency. I believe that the first step towards treatment and reform is to face up to the unvarnished truth, painful though this may be. Unless and until a process of catharsis is instituted – and here President Mubarak's administration has a vital role to play – there is no real hope for reform.

7. Liberation of the Media

Another major impediment to the instauration of democracy is the close control exercised by the present government over the so-called 'national' press and other mass media such as radio and television. A model well worth looking into here is the British Broadcasting Corporation, more familiarly known as the BBC. The presidency should place before the president of the republic the example of the BBC, whose organizational structure and method of operation I had occasion to study at close quarters in the course of several visits to its corporate headquarters. Since its inception, the BBC has been an autonomous body that remains quite independent from successive governments, in both its administrative structure and its editorial policy. The Egyptian presidency could draw several important lessons from the experience of the BBC, which is a superb example of a body that, though wholly owned by the state, is totally independent from the government and the party in power. In addition, the BBC is not dependent on the vagaries of the capitalist market for its livelihood; unlike broadcasting networks in countries such as the US, BBC radio and television do not broadcast commercials.

As to the press, either one accepts the viewpoint of certain members of the present government and the ruling party that the press is an information medium whose function is to support the regime and justify its policies – in which case one must accept the status quo, namely, a press that, though graced with the title 'national', is in fact a government organ controlled by the president of the republic, the chairman of the Shura Council (the upper house of parliament), and the minister of information, who select and appoint the editors-in-chief – or one recognizes that a press which serves as the mouthpiece of the government cannot serve as the watchful eye and critical mind of the nation – in which case one must accept that it has to undergo a basic transformation. Without serious efforts in this direction, the standard of the national press in Egypt will continue to decline, regarding both the editorial content of the newspapers and the calibre of their editors-in-chief, who can only be classified as civil servants or managers, but never as intellectuals or political writers. This sorry state of affairs has serious implications touching on the very integrity of the press as an institution whose primary responsibility is towards the public, a responsibility Egyptian national newspapers can hardly discharge while they remain as dependent on the ruling power as a hired hand is on his boss.

It would not be unduly harsh to say that most of those who write in the national press lack any intellectual or cultural depth. Sadly, the general cultural level of most journalists – with the exception of a few veterans belonging to the pre-totalitarianism generation – is most superficial. A quick comparison between the level of writing which graced the Egyptian press in the 1930s and 1940s, and the one to which the public are exposed in today's nationals, highlights the horror of the situation and the extent of the tragedy. Without going too deeply into the whys and wherefores of the present crisis in Egyptian journalism, another quick comparison may help cast some light on the issue. That comparison touches on the nature of relations between journalists of the pre-revolution era and public figures of the time, and the undue deference shown to their counterparts today by journalists of the national papers, who will queue submissively for hours at the door of this or that public official, forgetting that the pens they wield are far mightier than any powers vested in these officials.

8. Setting Priorities Right

If we contemplate what is written, spoken and broadcast in the political, media and cultural fields nowadays, we find that many members of the Egyptian intelligentsia, as well as those concerned with public affairs, share the following attributes:

- Although Egyptian, they are far more concerned with international and regional matters than they are with the reality that nearly 30 million of their compatriots live below the poverty line, in conditions that defy the imagination. Their skewed focus is particularly strange given that the challenge of poverty and the threat it poses to Egypt's national security should have been of such concern to Egyptian intellectuals as to leave very little room for any other issue, international, regional or even local.
- Although Egyptian, they are far more concerned with international and regional matters than they are with the declining standard of their country's educational institutions, which will determine the shape, quality, standard and future of less than the 20 million Egyptians who are today included in the country's educational system. Here too their order of priorities is strange.
- Although Egyptian, their concern with international and regional matters far outweighs their virtually nonexistent concern with the extreme danger posed by the declining standard of all but a few components of the religious establishment, the vast majority of which are actively working against modern trends, progress and civil society. There is no doubt that this too is very strange, given that some members of the religious establishment are so divorced from the realities of the age, from enlightened thinking, reasoning and plain common sense, as to constitute a real danger to the minds of Egypt's young, who, instead of forging a healthy connection with the age in which we live, develop a pathological alienation from it.

The conclusion to be drawn from all of the above is that the Egyptian people have been re-indoctrinated over the last decades to focus on priorities that are no longer local – that is, no longer Egyptian. In this connection, I recall what I heard on more than one occasion from prominent political personalities in the United States, who remarked on the strange obsession displayed by many of the Egyptians they meet with issues of an international and regional, rather than national – that is, Egyptian – nature. As someone who claims to be familiar with the way the Anglo-Saxon mind works, I know how bewildering my American interlocutors must have found this phenomenon, for pragmatism is the hallmark of the Anglo-Saxon mindset, which is shared by the British, Americans, Australians and Canadians.

The reason the phenomenon of giving precedence to external over internal affairs has become so widespread is the ascendancy of two ideological-cum-political movements which identify with it wholeheartedly. There is, first of all, the movement of political Islam, which resembles Marxism when it comes to its 'internationalist' dimension. Just as the communists believed they were part of a 'socialist international' that transcended national borders, so the Islamists believe in a 'Muslim international' that transcends national borders, a theory inimical to such concepts as 'the modern state', 'the nation' (as homeland) and 'nationalism'. Instead, they subscribe to the idea of the *umma*, or nation as community, not in the sense of people occupying a defined territory and united under one political system, not even in the sense of a group of people sharing a common origin, language and history, but in the sense of believers in one religion, wherever they happen to be located. Naturally, we are talking here of the Islamic nation. This is not what the great enlightened thinker and writer Ahmed Loutfy el Sayed, or his disciples, meant by the word *umma*, which referred exclusively to the Egyptian nation. It is no coincidence that he called the party he founded in 1907 the Umma Party, from which the founders of other political parties later emerged. Some became leaders of the Wafd Party, others of the Ahrar Dustoureyeen, others still became prominent independents.

The other movement that contributed to the shift in the focus of priorities is Arab nationalism. Suffice it to recall that the decision to abolish the name 'Egypt' and replace it with 'Southern Province' (of the United Arab Republic) in 1958 was welcomed by the Arab nationalists, for whom the word nation means the Arab nation. And so, thanks to the powerful influence wielded by political Islam and Arab nationalism on the minds of the Egyptian people, the focus of their attention shifted from what should have been their first priority, which is internal affairs, to external issues having no direct bearing on their interests or welfare.

I know some would argue that there is a dialectical relationship between Egypt's external role and its ability to strengthen the internal front. In reply, I would like to make two points. The first is that this argument is valid only in respect of political leaders. But when matters reach a point where the Egyptian intellectual is more outraged at the condition of Palestinian children than at the condition of Egyptian children, when he/she is more concerned with external affairs than with internal calamities, then we are facing a bizarre phenomenon that needs to be addressed. The second is that logic and history tell us that internal weakness inevitably translates into external weakness. Both Mohamed 'Ali and Egypt in the 1960s fostered dreams of aggrandizement. But their dreams were shattered because they tried to play external roles at a time when their respective internal fronts were exceedingly weak.

Having said that, however, I would like to make it clear that I am not calling on people to stop caring about what happens in the outside world, including the Middle East, but only to rearrange their priorities so as to become like the citizens of advanced states where domestic affairs absorb far more than half the interest of citizens and intellectuals alike.

There is no doubt that responsibility for this aberration lies squarely on the shoulders of three establishments that have shaped the Egyptian mindset since the 1950s: politics, the mass media and education. Given that the returns from education can only be felt in the long term, it is up to the political and media leaderships to play the main role in the short and medium term. What Egyptians need is not ideologies but tools with which to build their future. I believe the most effective tools in this connection are science and modern management techniques. Nowhere was the inability of ideology to build a better society more graphically illustrated than in the countries that adopted the ideology of Marxism, notably the former Soviet Union, which failed spectacularly to create decent living conditions for their citizens. It is to be hoped that no one will try out the ideology of political Islam on Egypt until they discover, as Eastern Europe discovered to its cost, that no ideology, whether Marxism, Arab nationalism or Islamism, can create a strong society or decent living conditions for its citizens.

Finally, one must recognize that Egyptians, as a government and a people, have reached a critical threshold of backwardness and weakness which they can only overcome by radically changing many of their systems and patterns. They need to take decisive action in respect of a losing public sector which stands at the root of all their economic problems; they need to bring radical reforms to the agricultural sector if they are to break the vicious circle that has transformed Egypt – in just thirty years – from a nation that was self-sufficient in food production, to one that has to import 60 per cent of its food requirements; they need to change the unhealthy relationship between employers and workers, and replace it with a normal and productive situation compatible with a free economy based on the interplay of market forces; they must, while not losing sight of the achievements of advanced Western societies in the areas of social security, pensions, unemployment insurance, health care, and so on, break the fetters of the restrictive labour legislations which are largely responsible for their present backwardness, and for the bloated and corrupt bureaucracy prevailing in Egyptian government departments. Once again, I repeat that unless they admit how appalling their present reality is and how imperative it is to transform it, unless they accept criticism of the fundamental principles by which they are governed and not only that of the secondary symptoms, the chances of breaking out of the present bottleneck are bleak.

Also, while all these reforms are essential, the need to enhance freedoms and consolidate democracy should head Egypt's list of priorities, coming even before the need for economic reform. For, as the prominent thinker Mr Khaled Mohamed Khaled[27] pointed out, democracy will lead to reform in all areas, including economic reforms, while the opposite is not true: economic reforms will not necessarily lead to democracy. Even though I have completely given up on the civil servants who are passing themselves off as writers in the national newspapers, I have boundless faith in the ability of a number of independent writers of the pre-totalitarian generation, such as Mustapha Amin,[28] Ahmed Baha' El Din,[29] Khaled Mohamed Khaled, Zaki Naguib Mahmoud,[30] Abdel Rahman El Sharkawy,[31] Ihsan Abdel Quddus[32] and Galal Hamamsy,[33] to defend freedom and democracy and to stand up to all attempts to curb or violate any public freedoms, in particular, freedom of thought and expression.

NOTES

1. See Chapter 2, note 1.
2. (1126–98). Arab philosopher from Andalusia, also theologian and polymath.
3. Readers interested in Ibn Rushd's influence on thirteenth-century Europe are referred to the chapter entitled 'Ibn Rushd and the Enlightenment' in Dr Murad Wahba's book, *Mullak al bakika al mutlaka* [The Holders of Absolute Truth] (1999), available at http://www.4shared.com/file/60456761/c59d98dd/___.html, pp.105–10.
4. See Chapter 6, section 3B.
5. The values of progress as seen by the author are exposed in Chapter 10 of this book.
6. (1929–90). Famous Egyptian journalist and novelist.
7. See Chapter 7, note 1.

8. (1872–1932). Egyptian poet who wrote on political and social commentary; called 'Sha'er el Nil' (poet of the Nile).

9. See Chapter 7, note 3.

10. See Chapter 2, note 5.

11. (1898–1989). Prominent Egyptian writer and playwright.

12. (1876–1924). Mustafa Lutfi al Manfalouty was an Egyptian essayist and novelist; he came from a family of ulemas and had reformist ideas.

13. (Died 1937). One of the pioneers of Arabic literature in the first half of the twentieth century.

14. (1889–1966). Egyptian political thinker and historian; founder of the modern study of history in Egypt and the Arab world.

15. See Chapter 8, note 2.

16. (1895–1971). Abdel Razzak el Sanhuri was an Egyptian legal professor and scholar; he drafted the first version of the Egyptian Civil Code in 1949; he also played a major role in drafting the Iraqi Civil Code. He was forced by Nasser to retire in 1954.

17. See Chapter 6, note 3.

18. (1873–1928). Abdel Khalek Sarwat Pasha was prime minister of Egypt from March to November 1922, and then from April 1927 to March 1928.

19. (1897–1964). Famous Egyptian painter.

20. (1891–1934). Famous Egyptian sculptor; considered the father of modern Egyptian sculpture.

21. (1892–1923). Egyptian singer and composer; he put the music to the Egyptian national anthem, and is considered the father of Egyptian popular music.

22. (1907–91). Famous Egyptian singer and composer.

23. (1886–1954). Egyptian author and historian.

24. (1892–1952). One of the great figures of Egypt's liberal era. He obtained three doctoral degrees, and therefore insisted on being called Doctors Zaki Mubarak. While his first doctoral thesis was on Al Ghazali, his second was on the Arabic prose of the fourth Islamic century (i.e. the tenth century AD); finally, his third doctoral thesis (1937) was on Sufism in Islam. The first and second doctoral degrees were obtained from what is today Cairo University; the second was obtained in 1931 from what is today Université de Paris II (La Sorbonne).

25. (1889–1949). Ibrahim Abdel Kader el Mazny was an Egyptian writer, poet and journalist. He mastered English perfectly well and translated several poems from English to Arabic, including the Fitzgerald's English version of Omar El Khayam's poetry, *The Quartet*.

26. Huge missiles that the regime of Gamal Abd Al-Nasser in Egypt used to parade, and repeatedly announced that these were the long- and medium-range missiles that would remove Israel from the face of the earth. Linguistically, Qaher means 'conqueror' and Zafer means 'victorious'. The father of this book's author used to mock these huge missiles (when they were paraded) by saying 'an excellent carpenter has done a very good job', i.e. suggesting that they were not real missiles, but huge maquettes (wooden models). His statement reflected the views of the pre-1952 (Egyptian revolution) generation on the socialist era of Nasser (1954–70).

27. A well-known Islamist who was among the first echelons of the Muslim Brotherhood's leadership in the late 1940s and early 1950s; considered by many to be a (relatively) moderate Islamist who had a very good sense of social considerations and justice.

28. (1914–97). Prominent Egyptian journalist; co-founder of *Akhbar El Yom* newspaper; one of the fathers of modern Arabic journalism.

29. (1927–96). Prominent Egyptian journalist; was chief editor of several important Arabic newspapers.

30. (1905–93). Egyptian pioneer of philosophical and literary enlightenment. He was described by Al Aqqad (see Chapter 2, note 5) as 'the philosopher of authors and author of philosophers'.

31. (1920–87). Famous Egyptian poet, novelist, journalist and Islamic thinker.

32. See Chapter 9, note 6.

33. One of the first journalists of *Akhbar al Youm* newspaper.

10

Perpetual Progress

1. PROGRESS HAS NO NATIONALITY

In the last forty years, fears of a cultural invasion have dominated the thinking of many in the Arabic-speaking societies. When the bipolar world order collapsed at the end of the 1980s and the world began to talk of an emerging phenomenon that is now widely known as globalization, the proponents of the cultural invasion theory adapted their language to the new terminology and began to talk of the globalization of cultures as a dangerous development which threatened to erode the Arab cultural specificity.

I have addressed this issue in many of my writings, and I came to the conclusion that only those with a meagre fund of cultural specificity have something to fear from the globalization of culture. Those standing on a solid foundation of cultural identity, with a cultural specificity derived from factors related to history and geography, such as Japan, need not fear the loss of their cultural identity under any circumstances. The examples some people give of the effects that the winds of change coming from abroad have had on Japan's cultural construct can all be classified as 'secondary issues' – eating fast food, wearing American clothes, and the like. But when it comes to human relations, to the high esteem in which old people are held, to family values and other intrinsically Japanese values, such as the Japanese understanding of work, Japan has not surrendered one iota of its cultural specificity, despite the fact that for the last sixty years it has been dealing extensively with the outside world.

But while there might be some justification for fears that the Arab cultural specificity will be unable to stand up to the onslaught of cultural globalization, this does not apply with regard to the values of progress, all of which find much to support them in the models of civilization from which specific cultural traits are derived. There is nothing in any of these models – the Egyptian, Arab, Islamic or Christian – that can be construed as running counter to values such as a respect for time, quality, universality of knowledge, teamwork, a culture of systems rather than a culture of individuals, or a belief that management is one of the most important instruments of success. Indeed, I would go as far as saying that these values were upheld and applied in the history of the Arabs hundreds of years before another chapter in humanity's civilizing process took them over and used them in creating a better life. There are those who would agree with me save when it comes to the value of pluralism, on the grounds that Islamic religious thinking is based on a 'unique model of righteousness'. This is an erroneous assumption which is belied by numerous Qur'anic texts, perhaps the most important of which reads as follows: 'And if thy Lord willed, all who are in the earth would have believed together' (Surah of Jonah, Verse 99). There are also many texts in the Sunna (the rules of life according to the Hadith, or teachings of the Prophet), extolling pluralism as one of the sublime values which all Muslims should strive to uphold.

How, then, can anyone allege that values of progress such as time, quality and even pluralism threaten the Arabs' cultural specificity? And yet that is the theme of an ongoing debate in their society which is both bizarre and humiliating. Those who argue against the adoption of values of progress, on the grounds that they run counter to the value system and cultural identity of Arabic-speaking societies, expect these instead to embrace values that can only drag society onto the road to backwardness and underdevelopment. This regressive trend is a relatively recent phenomenon in, for example, Egypt's modern history. For additional proof that the values of progress are compatible with Egypt's cultural specificity, one needs only to look at the last hundred years of its history. These were marked by periods of enlightenment during which most of the values of progress were far more present in the lives of Egyptians than they became after the beginning of what has been termed by some as a process of 'dismantling' Egyptian society.

The debate over cultural specificity versus values of progress takes me back to a period in the 1980s that I spent working in one of the fastest-developing countries in Southeast Asia, where the two largest ethnic communities, and hence the main sources of labour, were the Chinese and the Malay. The prevailing view at the time was that any economic establishment wishing to run an efficient and successful business had to recruit its staff from the Chinese community, whose members were diligent and hard-working and who, moreover, displayed a natural propensity for teamwork; the Malays, meanwhile, were generally regarded as lazy, slipshod and highly individualistic. This negative image of the Malay worker remained in place until one man came to lead a country – in which 90 per cent of its inhabitants belong to the ethnic group once maligned in the international labour market, the predominantly Muslim Malays – towards a miraculous recovery. In less than twenty years, Malaysia, whose people were mired in backwardness and stigmatized as lazy and inefficient, broke through the barriers of underdevelopment to gain worldwide recognition for the high quality of its products and services. With one of the fastest-growing economies in the world, Malaysia has come to embody all the values of progress, breaking the stereotype of the 'lazy Malay', and opening the eyes of the world to two inescapable truths.

First, that backwardness is not the result of a biological fatality but of circumstances, and, to the same extent that circumstances can change, backwardness can be overcome.

Second, that the values of progress can take root and flourish in any environment, Christian, Buddhist, Islamic or otherwise, and they are by no means exclusive to any specific environment.

The Malaysian experience can also be used to illustrate another truth, namely, that progress can go hand in hand with cultural specificity. Malaysia's strong cultural traditions relating to human relations, family relations and religious values have remained as constant since its economic takeoff as they were when it was a struggling underdeveloped country. The credit for Malaysia's economic miracle is sometimes attributed to its Chinese minority. Even if this were true, it means that progress can come about by 'contagion', which is not a bad thing. But this is an overly simplistic explanation for the Malaysian miracle. After all, the Chinese minority has always been around. The only new factor is the emergence of Mahathir bin Mohamed,[1] the man who wrought this amazing change in Malaysia's fortunes through visionary and efficient leadership.

2. PROGRESS: EXAMPLES

A. Time

An issue that has sparked an animated debate in the Arab society is the discrepancy between the value attached to time by citizens of advanced societies, and its value for the Arab citizens. Commentators offer different explanations for the phenomenon, the majority attributing the importance of time in advanced societies to the higher levels of discipline and organization displayed by the citizens of those societies. But this superficial view only skims the surface of a much deeper problem.

The more discerning and insightful commentators realise that the issue is symptomatic of a more complex problem, in which discipline, organization and punctuality are but manifestations of a profound difference in understanding, evaluating and appreciating time itself. In the more advanced societies, time is the framework in which plans are made and executed, projects are designed and launched – in fact, it is the framework for everything: ideas, projects, plans, programmes and reform movements, as well as economic, scientific, educational, cultural and social development. Anyone who is not aware of the value of the framework is necessarily unaware of the value of anything which that framework can encompass.

Strangely enough, there is a widespread belief in Arabic-speaking societies that venerating time, meeting deadlines and showing up for meetings at the appointed time is a question of temperament, an innate quality that one is either born with or not. This is a totally erroneous assumption. A well developed sense that time must be respected, appointments punctiliously observed and deadlines met; that all ideas, projects, plans and programmes must be set within specific time-frames; and that a cavalier attitude towards time and appointments detracts from a person's credibility, authority and ultimately his effectiveness – all these have nothing to do with temperament. It is not an individual's genetic make-up that determines their attitude towards time, but the general cultural climate prevailing in the society to which they belong.

Unfortunately, promptness and punctuality are regarded in the Arab society as idiosyncrasies displayed by an eccentric few who just happened to be born with a natural disposition to stick to schedules, in contradistinction to the laid-back attitude displayed by the vast majority of their fellow citizens.

And here we come to the crux of the matter. The measure of any society's development and progress does not lie in the wealth of which it disposes or the natural resources that it harbours, but in the value system to which its citizens subscribe, the mores by which the entire community, from the base to the summit, is governed. The most important of these values are a respect for time; a strong work ethic; a belief in the effectiveness of teamwork; an emphasis on developing human resources; and the adoption of an educational system based on promoting initiative and creativity rather than on teaching by rote, fostering a spirit of perseverance and encouraging people to strive for excellence, instilling the notion of universality of knowledge in young minds and, finally, promoting a spirit of healthy competition from the very start of the educational process.

Once this value system is in place, progress can be made. In its absence, or in the context of a value system that runs counter to these basic principles, a society is doomed to remain locked in backwardness. Rather than admit their own responsibility for the rut in which they find themselves, these societies tend to attribute their inability to move forward either to factors beyond their control, such as a lack of resources, or to external factors, such as a conspiracy hatched against them by foreign interests. Such self-delusion only serves to reinforce the negative features of such societies, for it is only by admitting to themselves that what holds them back is their own crippling inertia and their own lack of drive that they can hope to break the vicious cycle of backwardness.

Venerating time and placing all human, institutional and social activities within its framework is not simply a personal idiosyncrasy or an innate virtue enjoyed by some and not others; it is what distinguishes between two value systems: one that responds to the requirements of the age, and another that derives either from the antiquated cultural traditions of a primitive agricultural society or from a Bedouin culture. Students of the development of values in general and the values of progress in particular know that time did not acquire its high value, its status as the dividing line between progress and underdevelopment, until the advent of the Industrial Revolution. It was this watershed event which imposed a new understanding and appreciation of the importance and value of time and the need to observe it rigorously. Nowhere is the respect for time more graphically illustrated than in Switzerland – where trains run on schedules measured not in hours, or even minutes, but in seconds – in what is surely the highest possible expression of industrial values and the values of a service society. The information revolution and the requirements of the age of technology have further enhanced the value of time, which has come to be venerated with an almost religious fervour by those who believe it is the key to progress.

The value system of any society can be enriched with progressive values inculcated in the collective conscience by examples set by those at the summit of the societal pyramid. Conversely, if those expected to set an example fail to uphold the required values – including a respect for time – then it is virtually impossible for those at the base of the pyramid to take on such values as part of their cultural baggage. The influence of the upper echelons of society on the behavioural patterns of that society is recognized by the folk wisdom of all cultures. It is a theme that appears in several Arabic proverbs, such as 'People follow the religion of their king', 'A fish begins to putrefy at its head', 'It is the shepherd who guides the flock', and many more. In other words, if the values conducive to progress, including, of course, a well-developed sense of time, are not promoted by those holding positions of authority, such as senior public officials, cabinet ministers and economic and business leaders, they will never become part of the reference system of society. These values can only be disseminated from the top of the societal pyramid to its base and not the other way round, as those at the base have neither the clout nor the channels through which to impose their values as examples to be followed by society at large.

In the decade during which I served as CEO of one of the largest economic corporations in the world, with thousands of highly qualified employees drawn from some twenty countries working under my direction, I was able to ascertain at first hand the existence of a direct link between high levels of performance and a strict observance of time, an almost mystical belief in the importance of punctuality and of completing work assignments within the designated time-frame. Nor did this apply only to staff members. It was also true of the thousands of high-ranking political and economic personalities I met by virtue of my office; the more punctilious they were about keeping appointments and adhering strictly to schedule, the higher was their level of competence and performance – and the more intolerant they were of those who did not attach the same high priority to the time factor.

The nature of my job, which entailed doing business with people from different cultural backgrounds, made me realize that the whole concept of time varied from one culture to another. There were occasions, for example, when I had to terminate a contract for hundreds of millions of dollars because the other party had defaulted on its obligation to complete execution within an agreed deadline. If the defaulting party happened to be from the Third World, the decision would be derisively dismissed as an overreaction to a trivial matter; but it was accepted with resignation – if not good grace – when the other party happened to be from the West or from Southeast Asia, where termination is seen as the only possible response to a failure in meeting with agreed deadlines.

The different reactions to the example I have chosen to give reflect the very different appreciations of time between one culture and another. For Third World societies, time is of such little value that taking a person to task for being late for an appointment, or penalizing a contractor for failing to deliver works by an agreed date, is regarded with genuine surprise. In fact, being late has become a symbol of personal worth, a validation of one's importance in the scheme of things. After all, important people are so busy that they are entitled to be late, and whoever is lucky enough to be granted a slice of their valuable time must understand that waiting is par for the course. This phenomenon is turned on its head in advanced societies, where people running huge enterprises with budgets greater than the combined economies of all the Arab countries pride themselves on never being late for an appointment or running over schedule. In fact, they consider themselves in a constant race against time, often striving not only to meet agreed deadlines, but to even beat them.

I have learnt from experience that a lack of respect for time, whether it takes the form of showing up late for appointments or not completing assignments and projects within the agreed time-frames, condemns the individual, company or institution displaying this aberrant form of behaviour to failure, not only in the sphere of business but in all life aspects. Any exception or willingness to condone exceptions is seen as running counter to science, progress and the movement of history in advanced societies. There is a big difference between punctuality motivated by fear – which is sometimes the case in Third World countries – and punctuality as a way of life, the natural expression of an ingrained sense of the importance of time, and a recognition that unless schedules are rigorously observed and time frames respected, there can be no progress – which is the case in advanced societies.

In Third World countries, members of parliament are invariably late for meetings of the legislative assembly, which are usually chaotic affairs with members chatting among themselves, talking on their cellphones, using the time to catch up on their private businesses or engaging in side conversations with officials. However, when they are invited to a meeting attended by the head of state, these same parliamentarians show up well ahead of time, sit quietly in their seats and refrain from engaging in side conversations. Such uncharacteristic punctuality and discipline are not motivated by a respect for time as such or by a sense of occasion, but by entirely different considerations that will not be lost on the reader. The problem is that obsequiousness and fear cannot drive the wheel of progress and development forward.

A main reason for the lack of respect in Third World societies for the value of time and the failure to recognize its importance as one of the cornerstones of civilized behaviour and progress is the emergence of a new moneyed class in many of these societies. The members of this new class are for the most part poorly educated and largely uncultured, having built up their fortunes through political patronage and cronyism rather than by virtue of any special business, economic or scientific skills.

As their numbers grew and their political and economic clout increased, they became social trendsetters, a new source for the dissemination of negative values in society, including a lack of respect for time. The members of this new parasitical class, who acquired unimaginable wealth suddenly and in the complete absence of any cultural background whatsoever, have absolutely no notion of time being one of the principal values of civilization and progress. Moreover, the often dubious way they made their fortunes hardly qualifies them to serve as examples to be followed or role models to be emulated. How can we ask the young people to follow the example of the leaders of economic life in the country – the so-called businessmen – when they are the living embodiment of negative values in general, and of disdain for time in particular? There is also the fact that in a number of Third World countries, the class of businessmen and new rich has been infiltrated by the Mafia; how then can we expect them to serve as examples, or uphold positive values, including a respect for time? I have dealt closely with many of those who pass themselves off as business leaders in the Arab society. Unlike their international counterparts, the vast majority are characterized by a complete absence of managerial talent and by astounding cultural poverty, blatant political opportunism, and a lack of leadership qualities. Most had established their institutions and businesses on a basis of personal relationships rather than on management skills, proper economic use of state-of-the-art technology, or ability to administer services. In other words, they are totally unfit to fill the leadership role into which they have been thrust, or to serve as role models for new generations of young people.

Of all the points made in this chapter, the one that cannot be repeated often enough is that the top management of any enterprise cannot hope to run a successful and efficient business unless a respect for time is a basic feature of its make-up. That is not to say that a respect for time is a sufficient condition for efficient management, but it is certainly a necessary condition. Although a respect for time is perhaps the most important prerequisite for successful management, other features must also be present. As matters now stand, Arabic-speaking societies do not have a cadre of executive managers capable of achieving what to many may appear to be an impossible task, but which I believe is a goal well within the Arabs' reach, namely, attaining a degree of economic and educational development similar to the countries of southern Europe. This should proceed in parallel with the development of a rich cultural life, and the social peace that can guarantee to all the society to which Arabic-speaking people aspire: a stable, safe and thriving society, in which citizens will once again come to display the characteristics for which they have been famous throughout history: humanity, tolerance, kindness, patience, geniality and respect for others, far away from the violence, hatred and daily clashes between people, classes and the various component elements of society.

B. Systems versus Individuals

Some time ago, I was reading an article by a well-known writer when I was struck by his remarks about an Egyptian ambassador who had just been recalled from one of Egypt's larger embassies abroad. After heaping some probably well-earned praise on the ambassador, he quoted a highly-placed personality as saying that if it were up to him, he would have kept the ambassador in question on at the same embassy, regardless of the rotation system in force at the foreign ministry, because it was a shame to let the many contacts he had built up go to waste and have his replacement start from scratch. As a man interested in management and culture, I was shocked at this logic, not because it was wrong – indeed, it made sense from a practical point of view – but because it revealed a dangerous facet of the Egyptian mindset that has been forged over centuries under specific historical and cultural circumstances. The case of the ambassador is far from being an isolated incident. The same logic is invoked whenever a public official shines at his job; the same voices are raised to call for exceptions in the system to accommodate that particular individual. This graphically illustrates that the Arab mindset believes far more profoundly in the role of the individual than it does in the effectiveness of systems in which the individual is only one cog in a complex wheel of interactive and interdependent elements.

Having lived until the age of 25 in a purely Egyptian environment, it was not until I was exposed to different cultures that I realized how vast a difference separated the Egyptians' perception of the respective roles of the individual and the system from that of other societies, most notably those of northern Europe, where the exact opposite logic prevails. While placing a high value on the individual and devoting huge resources to ensuring his formation in the best possible manner, these societies place an even higher value on the system.

It is hard for most people in Arabic-speaking societies, who tend to attribute success, efficiency and the achievement of goals to the fortuitous presence of an outstanding individual in a specific post, to realize the disastrous consequences that can flow from such logic. To count on chance is to suspend all the rules of rationality, while to believe that an outstanding individual must remain in his post because his replacement will have to start from scratch is to give in to a problem rather than attempt to resolve it. The Arabs' approach to the issue is a reflection of the discontinuity of their organizational structures, and the lack of a coherent strategy governing trends and endeavours in their society. It also works against the social mobility that is essential, not only for the promotion of the middle class, but also for the promotion of society as a whole. Moreover, the approach carries within it the seeds of deeper problems, in that it proceeds from the premise that they are ready not only to pay the high price of dealing with the laws of chance, but even to accept whatever results come their way. This is in direct opposition to the rationale governing modern management science which, while believing in personal abilities and talents, believes more strongly in systems than in individuals.

The implication of linking achievements to the fortuitous presence of an outstanding individual in a specific post is that the Arabs allow the reins of their lives and future to be controlled by random chance which operates outside the realm of any rational laws. This approach is the exact opposite of that advocated by the French philosopher Jean-Paul Sartre,[2] who believed that the future does not exist as such, but is the product of our actions in the present. Stressing the importance of existence and the freedom and responsibility of the individual, he believed that the future begins in the here and now – more precisely, that what we do today will determine the features of tomorrow. But in the case of Arabic-speaking societies, on the contrary, they make no attempt to shape the features of their future through planning today. Rather, they count on the laws of chance to occasionally throw a few outstanding individuals their way – laws that are the direct antipode of the notions of system and planning.

This keenness on keeping outstanding individuals at their posts indefinitely is a result of one of the Arabs' main defects, which is the virtual absence of continuity and methodology in their development drive. For development to proceed as a consistent process rather than in fits and starts, mechanisms must be set in place to ensure continuity regardless of changes in names and faces. The argument invoked to justify keeping efficient functionaries at their posts beyond the pre-scribed period, which is that whoever replaces them will have to begin from square one, is a painful admission of the lack of continuity between generations of individuals. Adding impetus to this argument is the fact that in Arabic-speaking societies, no public official leaving his post will ever praise his successor, unlike his counterparts in the political, economic, cultural, educational and media institutions in advanced societies.

Another disadvantage of keeping the same individual at his post indefinitely, however outstanding that individual may be, is that it is not conducive to the social mobility that is the basis for positive inter-action in and the progress of any society, as well as a prerequisite for the growth of a strong and broad-based middle class that can lead that society. Moreover, the tendency to believe more in individuals than in the system exposes society to another, even greater, danger. While a culture of systems can keep destructive elements from occupying prominent positions, the same is not true in societies where a culture of individuals prevails. To the same extent that such a culture can promote outstanding individuals to positions of influence, it can also promote destructive and dangerous individuals. In the absence of an effective mechanism to prevent them from reaching a position of influ-ence in time – and time is of the essence here – these negative elements can wreak havoc.

In addition, the Arabs' infatuation with a culture of individuals is in direct contradiction with the basic premises of modern management sciences which, while drawing on the best qualities of the individual, give precedence to the big picture, that is to the framework in which the individual operates – in other words, to the system. In advanced societies, the basic building stone for progress and success is the sys-tem and not, as in the case of underdeveloped societies, a few – albeit exceptionally talented – individuals.

Defeating the Culture of Individuals. There is thus a clear dichotomy between the culture of individuals that has been all too manifest in the Arab society for tens of centuries, and the culture of systems which developed and put down deep roots in the West before moving on to many other societies that do not belong to Western civilization, such as Japan and other countries in Southeast Asia, as well as to various soci-eties in Central and Latin America. It is pointless at this stage to make value judgments or to address the issue from an accusatory perspec-tive. Rather, it should be placed in a historical perspective, and seen as the natural result of specific historical and cultural conditions. The question is whether a society governed by a culture of individuals can gradually transform itself into a society of systems. Judging from the experience of many societies, the answer is a resounding yes. These societies transformed themselves through a two-pronged approach, one that set its sights on short-term results, and another that aimed at effecting a radical long-term transformation. The first can be summed up in one word, 'leadership', or leading by example, which succeeded to a great extent in imposing a culture of systems on society. The greater achievement, however, was to entrench this culture deep into the collective psyche of society, a feat accomplished through the medium of 'education'. Only education is capable of bringing about a real transformation through curricula designed to minimize the dimensions of subjectivity and promote those of objectivity, the basis of any system or systems.

Vanquishing rivalry. Once a culture of systems takes root in society, the issue of specific individuals staying on at their posts is no longer a do-or-die proposition that takes on the dimensions of a military campaign as careerists scheme and manoeuvre to remain in place. In a culture of individuals, one of the main concerns of public officials is to fight off potential successors, making for an ugly relationship between incumbents and those whom they fear will replace them. That is the case in Arab-speaking societies, where rivalry for a position often degenerates into smear campaigns in which the predecessor and his successor are intent on blackening each other's reputation, and are not above resorting to slander and character assassination to achieve their end. This pattern of behaviour is symptomatic of a general cultural climate in which each official seeks out those who are qualified to step into their shoes at some point down the road, and goes all out to undercut their chances of succeeding.

As a result, one is left with a static situation in which genuine social mobility is replaced by what some call the rotation of elites, a process that is, by definition, opposed to change.

C. Quality

The idea of setting quality standards has become an independent field of study known as Quality Management (QM), which was added over the last four decades to the system of social sciences. Today, there are academies offering Quality Management as their only course of study. Although there is a great deal of literature on QM – the most famous being the works of Dr W. Edwards Deming, who is widely regarded as the father of this new discipline' – I do not want to go too deeply into the details and definitions of QM and its subject headings, which are quality management and control at the planning stage, quality management and control at the stage of execution, then a careful check of quality at the final stage. The application of the science of Quality Management and the spread of a quality culture are no more than reflections of a more fundamental issue, namely the presence of an effective process of social mobility that allows the best elements in society to reach the top of the societal pyramid. It is these elements that can spread quality consciousness throughout society and, eventually, lead it to adopt a culture of quality.

A society which does not allow for a process of social mobility favouring its best human elements, and which propels them into prominence, will never be governed by a culture of quality. In the absence of such a process, a culture of randomness and slipshod performance takes over, and the fickle hand of chance is left to determine the course of events – usually with disastrous consequences far removed from any notion of quality control.

As I mentioned in an earlier work entitled *Egyptian Transformation*,[4] untrammelled social mobility and the chain reactions it sets in motion are what allow the most able elements in society to occupy the leading positions in all walks of life. This creates a solid social pyramid that is developed over time by what some social scientists call social Darwinism, and that others (particularly those of a socialist formation) attribute to social mobility and the opportunity it provides for the best elements to reach the upper layers of the societal pyramid, and to contribute effectively in shaping society's present and future. Whatever the mechanism by which such a dynamic social pyramid is built up, at the end of the day, it remains the only way to propagate a culture of quality in society.

Conversely, a society whose composition does not allow for free social mobility leaves the door wide open for inept and mediocre elements to make their way to top positions in its organizations and institutions, thereby dealing a death blow to any prospect of a culture of quality, and creating a totally different cultural environment in which mediocrity holds sway; quality disappears, and virulent campaigns are unleashed against talented individuals by those with a vested interest in maintaining the status quo. They know that unless they work relentlessly to keep the rules of the game from changing, they are doomed to topple from the leading positions they occupy to positions more in keeping with their limited talents and abilities.

The question of the culture propagated by mediocre people in high places and the general climate they create should be a matter of grave concern for intellectuals and scholars who, more than anyone, are capable of seeing the big picture and understanding the negative implications of this phenomenon on society at large. There is no question but that the social and political structures of the Arab societies suffer from the ascendancy of mediocrity and the mechanisms set in place by its beneficiaries to keep themselves and others of their ilk in influential positions. The fallout from this phenomenon is reflected in the decline of values, ideals and ethics as well as in a shocking drop in their political, economic, cultural and educational standards.

A point worth making in connection with the notion of quality is that it is not linked to technological development, but to an abstract notion that perfection is a goal one strives to attain using whatever resources are available. This was the theme of a lecture I delivered at the Juran Institute for Quality Management in the United States,[5] in which I elaborated further on the idea that quality was a notion in the minds of certain outstanding individuals, and not the fruit of technology, which is itself the fruit of the intellectual prowess of outstanding individuals. To illustrate my point, I reminded my audience that quality control was a feature of the Ancient Egyptians, which found its most salient expression in the Great Pyramid of the Pharaoh Khufu. The amazing precision and unequalled grace of this remarkable monument to human ingenuity graphically illustrate that quality and high standards of performance have nothing to do with the stage of a society's technological development. Commenting on my lecture, the head of the Juran Institute remarked that I had chosen the best possible example to prove my point, as the logo of the Institute depicts an Ancient Egyptian worker chiselling in stone! Thus the biggest quality management institute in the world did not link quality to high technology, but chose to depict the notion with the image of an Ancient Egyptian craftsman using the most primitive technology to create perfection that defies time itself. In fact, the history of Ancient Egypt is filled with evidence that quality is a notion rather than anything else. A comparison between the pyramid built by Khufu and the two built by his father, the Pharaoh Snefru, shows how an enormous leap in the level of quality can be achieved in just a few years; in the absence of any significant technological breakthrough, this can only be explained in terms of a human cadre that took the vigorous pursuit of quality to a higher level.

D. Pluralism

If it is true that democracy is the greatest achievement of the human race since the march of civilization began, it is equally true that one of the wellsprings of democracy is pluralism. When people came to realize that diversity of creeds, opinions, viewpoints and tastes was one of the most important features of humanity, it was natural for political systems to incorporate and respect different trends without allowing any one of them, even if it enjoyed a strong or even absolute majority, to deprive the others of the right to differ with the majority's view, and to believe in other programmes, ideas, systems and theories.

Indeed, as the march of civilization progressed, the realization that pluralism was a basic feature of humanity evolved into a conviction that pluralism was a source for the enrichment of human life, as it expanded the horizons of creativity, innovation and renewal.

Although most members of the community of nations subscribe to the notion of pluralism as a basic component of their political systems, below the surface is a different reality in which the vast majority of people remain at a very primitive stage when it comes to really embracing this notion, and fully understanding and appreciating its meaning and benefits. This is as true of the most advanced societies (led by the United States) as it is of the less developed societies, including those of the Third World. There is mistrust and a mutual lack of understanding between the different civilizations, which renders the benefits and potential advantages of pluralism far fewer than they might otherwise have been. Some see the way out of this dilemma as the 'standardization' of the world – the replacement of diversity by a uniform model of civilization. Not only is this an unattainable goal, it is also the direct antithesis of the notion of pluralism. Moreover, any attempt to impose a universal norm would lay the ground for the spread of conflicts and clashes between civilizations, to the detriment of humanity as a whole.

Evidence of the vast legacy of mutual misunderstanding, mistrust and misconceptions between civilizations can be found in Western civilization's view of most Eastern civilizations, which is often based on fanciful notions totally divorced from reality. It can also be found in the often distorted perceptions that ancient civilizations have of the West, which tend to focus on the negative aspects of Western civilization while disregarding its positive aspects, even those which have benefitted the whole of humanity.

In recent years, the traditional mistrust between Orient and Occident was given new impetus with the emergence of a school of thought in the West in general and in the United States in particular, which believes that future relations between civilizations will be marked by clashes and conflicts, particularly the relationship between the West and Islam. The literature put out by this school of thought reveals a startling lack of understanding. Samuel P. Huntington's seminal book, *The Clash of Civilizations*,[6] and other similar works by authors such as Paul Kennedy[7] and Francis Fukuyama,[8] are closer to journalistic articles than they are to scholarly works based on a sound knowledge of the subject matter. In fact, Huntington's book is an expanded version of an article he wrote originally for the American quarterly *Foreign Affairs*.[9] Moreover, the authors of these works lack the vision that would enable them to see a mechanism which could replace the scenario of inter-civilization clashes with a scenario of dialogue between civilizations. That is not to say that the scenario of a clash of civilizations can be altogether excluded, but only that dialogue is possible if the vision exists and if serious efforts are made to transform it into reality.

Contemporary political discourse is peppered with references to democracy, human rights, general freedoms and pluralism. But raising these slogans is one thing; applying them is another. Nobody denies that these are noble values representing the highest stage, yet in the march of civilization, the fact is that the way they are translated into reality leaves much to be desired. This is particularly true of the value of pluralism. For example, while the West raises the banner of pluralism some of its citizens raise the banner of standardization. This confusion leaves a bewildered world convinced that humanity has a long way to go before it can claim to have genuinely adopted these values.

If pluralism means that a diversity of trends, creeds, cultures, tastes, opinions and lifestyles is a basic feature of human life and a source of its enrichment, it follows that one should strive for 'unity through diversity'. This entails expanding a culture of respecting 'Otherness', provided that this applies to all parties simultaneously and on a basis of parity. Respecting 'Otherness' is in direct contradiction with the idea of standardizing the world. Fortunately, this idea is not advocated by the West as a whole, and has not been taken up by Western Europe. It is an exclusively American notion based on nothing but America's cultural poverty.

E. Criticism and Self-Criticism … or 'The Floor is for Critical Minds'
I have long believed Immanuel Kant's famous statement, that criticism is the most important building tool devised by the human mind, to be the cornerstone of a healthy and dynamic educational/cultural environment. The analogy of the German philosopher's aphorism in Eastern literature is Omar ibn al Khattab's statement, 'Blessed is he who shows us our defects',[10] by which he calls on God to bless those who open our eyes to our defects through the medium of criticism.

After I had embraced the notion that a cultural climate which promotes critical faculties and celebrates critical minds is a prerequisite for a society's development and progress, I had the opportunity to work for twenty years in one of the ten largest economic corporations in the world. The experience allowed me to see this notion put into practice every day. With a history going back over a century, the corporation I worked for had its own internal culture, and it never ceased to amaze me that every single meeting, discussion and seminar in which I participated during my tenure embodied the axiom that criticism is the most important building tool devised by man. It did not occur to anyone to hold back from criticizing ideas, plans, programmes and projects, not only before, but during and even after their execution, in order to minimize the negative and maximize the positive aspects of performance in future. Nor was the right to criticize vested exclusively in the upper echelons of the organizational structure; it was a right available to and actively exercised by every thinking person in the firm. And it is from the collective efforts of critical minds that success and distinction are achieved.

For criticism to become an effective mechanism deployed in a constant quest for excellence by pinpointing whatever is negative as a prerequisite for minimizing it in future, and identifying the positive aspects of any idea, process, or performance with a view to maximizing them, it must operate in a general climate in which every member of society is familiar with the notion of objective – hence constructive – criticism. It is a type of criticism which differs in spirit, motivations and aims from the subjective criticism found in some cultures, where criticism is often used as a weapon of attack, revenge and defamation, to further personal agendas or settle old scores. The blame for this aberration lies squarely on the shoulders of a general cultural and educational climate which fails to develop the critical faculty in young minds, or to promote the notion that criticism should be used as a rational, objective tool to serve the general interest, and not private interests.

It is not surprising that societies governed by a general cultural climate in which pluralism is accepted and respected should be better equipped to use objective criticism as a means of optimizing all aspects of life than societies which do not tolerate any dissenting opinion or any departure from the norm. In such a monistic climate, there is no room for the sort of constructive and objective criticism that targets subjects and not individuals. Nor is it surprising that societies which I have previously called societies of systems, not individuals, should also be better equipped to deploy constructive criticism as a weapon against objective shortcomings.

There is a strong link between a culture of constructive criticism and social mobility. In a society marked by an active process of social mobility which allows for a dynamic process of job rotation in general, and among elites in particular, there is a wider scope for planting the seeds of a culture of constructive criticism. The opposite holds true in a closed society where, in the absence of real social mobility, hanging on to the job becomes a do-or-die proposition. This blurs the distinction between what is objective and what is subjective, and creates a climate that is inimical to objective criticism.

I also believe in a strong link between the values of mediocrity referred to in the previous section here on 'Quality' and the difficulty of propagating a culture of constructive criticism. People of mediocre abilities are aware that they cannot survive in a climate of constructive criticism that would expose their limited skills and talents. And so they ferociously oppose the introduction of a system of performance evaluation, based on objective criteria, by working actively against the dissemination of a culture of constructive criticism.

In the final analysis, the diffusion of a general cultural climate which welcomes and encourages constructive criticism and educates people on the merits of developing their critical faculties and the enormous benefits this will bring to society as a whole is one of the most important values of progress. And like all the other values of progress, it can only become generalized throughout society in the immediate term by a determined effort on the part of those in positions of leadership to set an example, and in the long term by means of educational curricula designed to inculcate its importance in people's minds.

F. Knowledge

One of the most salient features of the globalization process has been the unrestricted flow of information between the various sectors of the global community, not least in the domain of science. Even those who reject some of the aspects of globalization cannot deny the positive effect it has had in opening up channels of communication between the many institutions working in every branch of science and scientific research. This is particularly true in the field of applied science and technology, where universality of knowledge has become an established feature. The main reason why this feature has acquired such importance is the strong relationship in advanced societies between scientific research and life in general – and economic life in particular. It is also the reason why the field of Research and Development (or R & D, as it is known), which is concerned primarily with the practical application of scientific findings, has come to eclipse in importance the field of scientific research proper, which, in the traditional meaning of the word, is almost totally divorced from life functions.

As advanced societies removed science from behind the high enclosures of universities and research centres, and put many of its branches to work in the service of their life/economic/social functions, universality of knowledge in the service of life functions became an inescapable fact of life in the world of applied sciences. The importance of R & D is reflected in the size of the budgets it commands, which far exceed those allocated to pure scientific research. And while the latter is subsidized for the most part by states and academic institutions, most R & D is funded by private economic institutions driven by the need to stay ahead of the competition. Anyone working in an industrial, commercial or services sector today must seek out the latest technology in that sector, wherever it may have been developed, and put it to use in enhancing performance, expanding activities and maximizing returns; hence the growing relevance of the notion of universality of knowledge.

It would be no exaggeration to attribute much of the credit for promoting the notion of universality of knowledge to the unique experience of post-war Japan. Like the fabled phoenix, Japan rose from the ashes of its crushing defeat in the Second World War[11] to assert itself as an economic giant on the world stage, thanks largely to its determination to seek out the latest achievements in science and technology in every part of the world, thoroughly assimilate their inner workings and put them to use in remarkable ways. Things are not quite so simple in the field of social science, where outlooks are conditioned by cultural factors and considerations. And yet, the notion of universality of knowledge is gaining ground in certain branches of social science, albeit not at the same pace as in the domain of applied science. For example, modern management, human resources and marketing sciences, and many other economic disciplines, have managed to cross borders and apply the notion of universality of knowledge in practice. This may be due to the fact that they are largely culture-free. But even those branches of social science with a strong cultural dimension are being infiltrated to some degree by the notion of universality of knowledge.

Resisting the notion may appear to some, particularly in the Arab world, as a natural feature of ancient civilizations. It is not so. Consider the case of China, one of the oldest civilizations in the world. Among the most passionate adherents to the values of progress in general, and the notion of universality of knowledge in particular, are the Chinese communities of Southeast Asia, and it was this which allowed them to play an instrumental role in the remarkable progress achieved by the region. Then there is the case of Japan, as previously mentioned, another ancient civilization which stands as one of the foremost examples of the values of progress in action, most notably the universality of knowledge. There is also India, an ancient civilization which, despite its many social problems, is one of the few Third World countries whose scientific institutions can hold their own with the best in the world. By keeping the bridges of scientific and technological research open between itself and the rest of the world, India has been able to score impressive achievements in many fields, notably in the arms industry and in computers and information technology. These examples attest to the ability of ancient civilizations to adopt the notion of universality of knowledge without threatening their own cultural specificity.

How, then, can the reluctance of Arabic-speaking societies to partake of the benefits of universality of knowledge be explained? I believe it is due to the lamentable deterioration of their educational institutions and scientific research centres, as a result of the subjugation of education and science in these societies to political life. Not surprisingly, this has cut them off from scientific progress in the rest of the world, smothered the spirit of creativity and turned them into stagnant entities totally cut off from scientific research in all branches of applied and social sciences. As a result, there is a near-total Arab absence in the domain of scientific achievements and creative research in these fields.

G. Work and Modern Management

If the six values mentioned earlier are among the values of progress which must be firmly planted in a society's general, cultural, and educational environment as a prerequisite for that society's development, they are also among the most important values on which modern management concepts are based. Thus these values, which will be addressed here, should not be seen in isolation from the values of progress addressed earlier in the chapter, as all the values together constitute the conceptual framework governing work in the modern workplace.

1. Teamwork. In the course of the many years I spent working in an environment that was international in the real sense of the word, bringing together as it did thousands of people from different countries and with widely divergent cultural backgrounds, I had many opportunities to see how the concept of teamwork is totally alien to most Arabs.

Unlike their colleagues from Asia, notably those from Japan or China where the spirit of teamwork is particularly vibrant, or from other parts of the world, such as Europe which also has a tradition of teamwork, the majority of Arabs with whom I worked found it extremely difficult to subsume their individuality in collective endeavours as members of a team. The ego issue often led to clashes, as each individual sought to ensure that he would get the credit for any success and others the blame for any failure. None was prepared to have his contribution regarded as just one component element in a collective endeavour. In hundreds of cases, this attitude led to crisis situations, with a disgruntled employee demanding that either he/she be taken off the team or that so-and-so be dropped – or else! This was in stark contrast to the attitude displayed by others belonging to different cultural backgrounds, such as the British, Asians and Germans with whom I worked, and only served to confirm how hard most Arabs find it to put their egos aside and accept thanks for a job well done when they are not singled out for praise.

Given that modern management sciences are based on a set of fundamental values, teamwork being among the most important, applying modern management techniques to large numbers of Arabs is a difficult proposition, unless they happen to be working abroad, in which case they have no choice but to submit docilely to the prevailing system of work, or lose their jobs. Many expatriate Arabs succeed brilliantly in their chosen field of expertise. All too often, however, their individualistic streak takes over, and they attribute their success exclusively to their own innate talents, conveniently forgetting that these talents would not have flourished as they did had it not been for the healthy environment which imposed on them the modern values of work, and brought out the best they had to offer.

In this connection, I recall what a professor at the California Institute of Technology said to me at the end of 1999:

> Ahmed Zeweil[12] is, by any standards, a prodigious scientist. But one should remember that seventeen people working in the same institute in which he works won Nobel prizes for their contributions to science. The moral to be drawn here is that the 'miracle of the system' is not only equal to, but even surpasses, the 'miracle of the individual', although both must be present at the same time in order for the required result to be achieved.

This view has been echoed by Ahmed Zeweil himself, who never tires of praising the 'team' without which he could not have achieved what he did. The Nobel laureate has also praised the 'working environment' in his institute, which he says deserves much of the credit for his 1999 Chemistry Prize. But as members of a 'culture of individuals', Egyptians tend to forget all aspects of the story and focus on the individual, because for over fifty centuries, from the time of the Pharaohs on, the Egyptian mindset has been conditioned by the cult of the individual. The system has no place in their scheme of things, even though it is the primary engine for progress and human achievement. The only mechanisms by which this defect in their make-up can be cured, are, as previously stated, leadership (as a tool of development in the short term), and modern education (as a tool of development in the medium and long term).

The word 'leadership' here is not just a vague and abstract term; it also denotes a modern manager formed in accordance with the requirements and culture of modern management sciences, which make every top executive responsible for managing work in their enterprise according to a system that groups employees into harmonious teams whose members complement one another, as opposed to the top executive who promotes individualism and factionalism by requiring each person in the establishment to owe allegiance to him/her personally. One of the most important tasks of a manager, formed and trained according to the spirit, culture, requirements and techniques of modern management sciences, is to foster a team spirit in his/her establishment. Unfortunately, most executives in the Middle East tend to promote a very different spirit in which employees are islands isolated from one another, and in communication only with the employer. This is a source of personal power for the top person, but it comes at the expense of the collective good, and does nothing to promote the spirit of teamwork that is one of the fundamental values of modern management science.

The negative culture which prevails in the Egyptian workplace derives in large part from the virtual absence of management education, in addition to the fact that most businesses are run by 'bosses' rather than by contemporary executive managers. It is further encouraged and conditioned by the culture of the Egyptian village, where for decades the *omda*, or village headman, has maintained his grip over village affairs by ensuring that the only channels of communication are between his constituents and himself. Any other pattern is frowned upon as a violation of the personal loyalty they owe to his person, and a direct challenge to his authority. All these factors conspire against the adoption of the values of modern management, including the important role assigned by contemporary management sciences to the executive manager. Indeed, most people find it difficult to understand just what the function of an executive manager is. On the surface, he/she does not appear to do much; but the truth is very different. An executive manager can be likened to an orchestra conductor who is required to ensure, at one and the same time, the high performance capability of each orchestra member taken separately, and the high quality of their collective performance as one team.

Thus, in the ten years I was responsible for projects worth billions of dollars, my days were not crowded with appointments and meetings, and my desk was not covered in paperwork, even though I was handling a daily volume of work running into well over 100 million dollars; while others who were running businesses and projects amounting to less than 1 per cent of the volume and value of the projects for which I was responsible were drowning in meetings, paperwork and files. I believe this was because they spent much of their time doing work that should have been done by others. Because they believed neither in teamwork nor in delegating authority, they ended up spending three-quarters of their time wading through mountains of unnecessary paperwork. Despite these strenuous efforts, however, the final results they achieved were at best mediocre and, more often than not, disgraceful.

Disseminating a culture which values teamwork begins with the formation of a human cadre of contemporary executive managers who understand what being a boss entails in the modern sense of the word, not in its pharaonic or medieval sense; when the top man was everything and his assistants were nothing. Without an administrative revolution in this field, any attempts to reform the working environment in Egypt and the other Arabic-speaking countries and make it more amenable to the notion of collective work and the spirit of teamwork are doomed to fail, because the heads of administrative organizations have a vested interest in maintaining the status quo, so that they can continue to keep all the reins of authority in their hands and take full credit for whatever success is achieved.

If the development of a high-calibre human cadre of executive managers capable of leading by example is an essential condition for development in the short term, what is required in the medium and long term is an educational revolution that will develop a strong work ethic in future generations, educate them in the importance of collective work, and promote the spirit of teamwork at every stage of the educational process. Both targets must be achieved if Egypt is ever to move from the culture of individualistic work inherited from pharaonic times to the work culture prevailing today, in which teamwork is used as a mechanism to maximize output by drawing on the collective minds, abilities and experience of the members making up the team.

Over two decades ago, I went to Switzerland to study the latest modern management techniques at the International Management Institute of Geneva University,[13] the largest specialized institute of its kind in Europe. The experience was a culture shock, as I found myself having to adjust to a system of learning very different from the one I was used to. Indeed, at first I thought I had made a mistake in registering for the course, which cost hundreds of thousands of dollars, and that I had been misinformed about how good the institute was. In the academic environment where I obtained my graduate and postgraduate degrees from an Egyptian university, the professor was the transmitter of knowledge and the students were passive receivers. The situation was very different at the institute, where the professor would begin each class by bringing up a particular theme or problem that was to be addressed by the students. These would then be divided into working groups, and each was sent off to a separate room. The groups were given a set time to study the problem, use the library for research, and come up with a report representing the collective views of their members. All the members of the group contributed equally to the report, and then chose one amongst them to present it on their behalf.

It was a technique of teaching that at first filled me with dismay, and I wondered why we were spending so much to receive such a meagre education. But over the following weeks and months, I gradually came to realize that it was in fact a highly sophisticated technique designed to develop leadership qualities and produce a human cadre capable of leading the world in every field. Contrary to the educational technique with which we are all too familiar, and which produces submissive followers trained to suppress their creative impulses while indulging their streak of destructive individualism, the technique employed at the institute produced innovators and believers who displayed a highly developed *esprit de corps*. This educational environment is what produces the best elements in any working environment. After all, what is work but a continuation of the early stages of education? The workplace is where the final output of the educational system – the individual – eventually ends up, and his/her performance in the workplace is as negative or positive as the education he/she received.

Accordingly, collective work or teamwork is a phenomenon linked to a society's cultural values, and some societies show a greater inclination for teamwork than others. Two of the leading examples are China and

Japan. According to management and QM scientists, these societies show a marked propensity for teamwork. However, it is an acquired characteristic, not a natural one, built up through their cumulative cultural experience. A yardstick that can be used to measure the extent to which a society has adopted the value of teamwork is the management techniques followed by that society's governmental and economic institutions. Another is the philosophy and technique of its educational system. The example set by the executive leaders in society can be instrumental in developing the spirit of teamwork. There is also a link between teamwork and the level of democracy in society. The greater the margin of democracy is, the better the prospects of making teamwork an essential component of a society's work ethic are. In an undemocratic society, the opportunity for advancement is restricted, and upward mobility in an organization is either slow or inexistent. This does not create a favourable climate for the development of a team spirit.

What we have here is a problem for which there is not one reason and not one cure; it is a multidimensional problem entailing a multilateral approach. As the German-born American political sociologist Herbert Marcuse[14] pointed out thirty years ago, the theory of the 'unidimensionality of cause'[15] has collapsed in all spheres of human thinking.

2. Human Resources. If management is the nerve centre of success in all the institutions of advanced societies, the optimal use of human resources is the backbone on which the success or failure of management rests. Human resource sciences have branched out to cover many areas, such as employee recruitment, selection and training, performance appraisal, human resources and organization, discovering leadership qualities, and other areas related to one of the most important fields of modern management, namely human resource management.

Modern human resource sciences proceed from a number of fundamental premises, such as the belief that in every person on earth there exists a 'gap' between his/her actual performance and his/her potential performance, and that it is one of the main tasks of management to discover that gap and work to overcome it by placing an individual in the position best suited to his/her abilities, temperament and personality within the organizational structure, and also through constant training.

Another fundamental premise is that any individual belongs to one of two basic groups made up respectively of specialists and generalists. Both groups are equally important, and both must be present in any successful and thriving organization.

Yet another is the need to make a basic distinction between potential and performance. While standards and rates of performance can be raised, all that can be done in respect of potential is to discover whether or not it exists. One of the principal tasks of top management in modern organizations is to discover early on those with a high potential, in order to elevate them to leading positions and to devise the required training programmes to hone their potential and imbue it with professionalism. Human resource sciences also attach a great deal of importance to the issue of motivation, whether in the material or moral sense.

The role of the 'chief' in a modern establishment differs from his/her role in a traditional bureaucracy, where he/she concentrates most of the centralized power in his/her hands and, over the years, transforms his/her fellow workers into an army of followers. In enterprises applying the techniques of modern management science, thus based on delegation, he/she does not involve him/herself in the day to day workings of the enterprise, leaving him/herself free to focus on strategic planning. In a sense, as I said before, his/her role is closer to that of an orchestra conductor than a military leader.

While traditional bureaucracies create followers, modern management seeks to create a cadre of human resources whose members are believers in the mission and aims of the establishment in which they are working. The sense of identification with the work organization is reflected in the quality of the on-the-job performance of the true believer, who sees the job not simply as a duty, but as a medium of self-expression and a source of personal gratification. In modern management terminology, this phenomenon is known as 'ownership' – that is, ownership of the moral returns of success at work.

In short, modern management does not regard human resources as machines, but as the key to success or failure. As such, they are entitled to enjoy the benefits and glory of the success they were instrumental in achieving. According to this view, there is no more effective engine for the advancement and success of an organization than the people working in it. This view is not the prevailing one in underdeveloped societies, where little attention is paid to creating an environment that encourages people to work and give their best. The opposite holds true in advanced societies, where the importance of the human element in moving the wheel of progress forward is widely recognized. The wealth of nations is not measured in terms of their natural resources or the riches they have amassed in the past, but in the quality of their human resources. This asset is built up through a process of planning and meticulous application of systems designed to discover the best in people, develop their potentialities to the full, and provide them with motivation.

3. Delegation. Modern management science tries to utilize each person in the best possible way. To that end, it attaches great importance to discovering latent abilities and to training and motivation, in the belief that enabling each individual to realize his/her full potential and allowing the free interplay of ideas is a source of enrichment not only for work, but for life in general. Advanced societies discarded the model of centralized management applied for long decades in the work establishment, which some believe they imported from the military establishment, when experience proved that it hindered the development of individual potential. That is why delegation has become one of the most important instruments of successful management today. Delegation is a reflection of the values I mentioned earlier, which lead to transforming work groups from armies of followers to teams of believers and create an environment conducive to innovation and creativity.

In a modern management system where top managers delegate their authority to others, the role of the manager can be likened yet again to that of an orchestra leader who does not play each instrument him/herself, but who directs others to play their best as an ensemble. In some modern establishments, the degree of delegation is such that the manager appears to have no work at all. This is, of course, a fallacy, as he/she is responsible for strategic planning, not for carrying out work that others can do as well as – and usually better than – he/she can. It would be safe to say that an establishment run according to all the values of modern management except for delegation is doomed to fail, because delegation is the translation of all these values into practice. However, delegation and training must go hand in hand; delegation without training cannot hope to succeed.

4. Marketing. The difference between countries which achieved remarkable progress in the economic field (through manufacturing a product or providing a service and then, at a later stage, through information technology) and those which spent billions on 'industrial arsenals' at the expense of real economic development, is that the activities of the former were focused on the end product, i.e. on 'marketing', while the latter's activities were focused on the initial process, i.e. on 'production'. Modern management science recognizes that a production-driven approach can only lead to failure and bankruptcy, while an approach that is marketing-driven is the best guarantee of success and growth. The truth of this axiom is corroborated by the huge discrepancy between the economies of the Eastern European countries (before the collapse of the Eastern bloc in the 1980s), which were production-driven, and those of Western Europe, which are marketing-driven.

If management is the secret for the success (or failure) of societies in general and economies in particular, marketing is the brains of management, in the sense that a successful management is one whose strategic thinking, business philosophy and internal mechanisms are marketing-driven.

While the importance of marketing as an essential value for the successful management of any enterprise cannot be overstated, its own success is contingent on the adoption of other values of progress. One such value is 'universality of knowledge'.[16] There can be no successful marketing in a closed environment shut off from the outside world. How can people hope to successfully market anything on a wide scale if they do not know enough about their competitors, international markets, the demands of those markets, and the cultures of the prospective buyers of their products or services? Another value that goes hand in hand with marketing is pluralism. How can anyone have one unique model for everything (the opposite of 'pluralism') and succeed in marketing, which is based on the highest objective of quality management science – to meet the expectations and satisfy the needs of the recipient of a product or service?

NOTES

1. (Born 1925). Fourth prime minister of Malaysia from 1981 to 2003.
2. (1905–80). French existentialist philosopher.
3. (1900–93). American professor, lecturer, consultant and statistician; he played a major role in improving production in the US during the Second World War. From 1950 he also taught management, quality and sales in Japan.
4. Please see author's book (in Arabic) *Al tahawol al massiry* [The Fateful Transformation], 1st edn (Cairo: Egyptian Lebanese Publishing House, 1993).
5. International consulting company founded in 1979 where training and consulting services in quality improvement and management are offered.
6. Huntington's theory about the clash of civilizations was first published in an article in 1993, then expanded into a book in 1996. See *The Clash of Civilizations and the Remaking of World Order* (New York: Simon and Schuster, 1996).
7. (Born 1945). British historian specializing in international relations.
8. (Born 1952). Author of many books, including *The End of History and the Last Man* (New York: Simon and Schuster, 1992).
9. American journal on international relations, published by the Council on Foreign Relations.
10. Omar Ibn el Khattab is the second Caliph who ruled the early Muslim State only two years after the death of Prophet Mohamed. Omar ruled for slightly less than eleven years and was assassinated, as were his two successors, Othman and Aly. Omar died in 644 AD.
11. See Chapter 3, note 1.

12. (Born 1946). Egyptian American scientist; earned the Nobel Prize in Chemistry in 1999.
13. Established in 1927.
14. (1898–1979). German philosopher and sociologist.
15. See Herbert Marcuse, *One-Dimensional Man* (Boston: Beacon, 1964).
16. See Chapter 10, section 2E

Epilogue

The Arabic-speaking societies refuse to join in the march towards modernity and progress. This refusal, in my opinion, is the product of three imprisonments, namely (1) the imprisonment of a widely spread anti-modernity and anti-integration religious wave; (2) the imprisonment of entirely out-dated educational systems; and (3) the imprisonment of undeniable anti-otherness misconceptions. I believe that the systematic rejection of modernity and progress which has resulted from these three imprisonments is the direct cause for the confrontation between a large number of Arabic-speaking people and the rest of humanity, a phenomenon which keeps the Arab Culture, people and mentality unable to integrate in the march of civilization based on progress and modernity. These societies need to engage with self criticism, and agree to adopt the values of civilization and progress discussed in this book; only then can they aspire to overcome the obstacles imprisoning them in their cocoon, and achieve modern development and progress in their diverse fields of life.

Bibliography

Abdel Malek, Anwar, *Égypte, société miltaire* [Egypt, Military Society] (Paris: Éditions du Seuil, 1962).

Al-Ghazali, Abu Hamid, *Tahafut al falasifah* [The Incoherence of the Philosophers]. First published in the eleventh century – available at http://www.ghazali.org/works/taf-eng.pdf.

El Sayed, Ahmed Loutfy, *Al siyasah* [translated version of Aristotle, *Politics*] (Cairo: Dar al kotob al misriyah, 1947). Written c. 1917.

El Sayed, Ahmed Loutfy, *Qessat hayati* [The Story of My Life] (Cairo: Kitab al hilal, 1962).

Engels, Friedrich, *The Conditions of the Working Class in England in 1844* (Germany: Leipzig, 1845).

Fukuyama, Francis, *The End of History and the Last Man* (New York: Simon and Schuster, 1992).

Hegel, Georg, *The Science of Logic* (Nüremberg/Heidelberg/Berlin: 1811, 1812 and 1816, revised 1831).

Heggy, Tarek, *Afqar Marxia fi al mizan* [Marxist Ideas in Balance] (Fes: Al Nasr Publishing House, 1978).

Heggy, Tarek, *Al sheyou'eya wal adian* [Communism and Religion] (Cairo: Dar Nahdat Misr, 1980).

Heggy, Tarek, *Tajribati ma'al marxia* [My experience with Marxism] (Cairo: Dar al Shorouk, 1983).

Heggy, Tarek, *Critique of Marxism* (Cairo: Dar al Shorouk, 1992); 2nd edn retitled *The Imperative Fall of Socialism* (Cairo: Merit Publishing House, 2009).

Heggy, Tarek, *Al tahawol al massiry* [The Fateful Transformation] 1st edn (Cairo: The Egyptian Lebanese Publishing House, 1993).

Heggy, Tarek, *Qiyam al taqaddum* [The Values of Progress] (Cairo: Dar el-Ma'aref, 2001).

Huntington, Samuel, *The Clash of Civilizations and the Remaking of World Order* (New York: Simon and Schuster, 1996).

Hussein, Taha, *Hadith al arbe'aa* [The Wednesday Talk] (Cairo: Dar al Ma'aref, 1925, 1926 and 1945), also available at http://www.fomscu-forum.com/vb/showthread.php?t=8211.

Hussein, Taha, *Mustaqbal al thaqafa fi misr* [The Future of Culture in Egypt] (Cairo: Dar al Maᶜaref, 1938).

Ibn Rushd, *Tahafut al tahafut* [The Incoherence of the Incoherence] (First published c. 1180 – available at http://www. muslimphiloso phy.com/ir/tt/).

Khalil Gibran, Gibran, *Al ᶜawassef* [The Storms] (Cairo: Manshurat al hilal al qahiriya, 1920). English edition titled *Storm*.

Machiavelli, Niccolò, *Il Principe* [The Prince] (Florence: Antonio Blado d'Asola, 1532).Written in 1513.

Marcuse, Herbert, *One-Dimensional Man* (Boston: Beacon, 1964).

Marx, Karl and Engels, Friedrich, *Manifest der Kommunistischen Partei* [The Communist Manifesto] (London, 1848).

Nietzsche, Friedrich, *Thus Spoke Zarathustra* (Chemnitz: Ernst Schmeitzner, 1883–85).

Shawki, Ahmed, *Aristotle* (Cairo: 1923). A poem.

Stewart, Desmond, *The Men of Friday* (London: Heinemann, 1961).

Stewart, Desmond, *Great Cairo: Mother of the World* (London: Rupert Hart-Davis, 1969).

Wahba, Murad, *Mullak al hakika al mutlaka* [The Holders of Absolute Truth] (1999), available at http://www.4shared.com/file/60456761/ c59d98dd/___.html).

Index

Names of publications beginning with the letters 'A' or 'The' will be filed under the first significant word. Page references to endnotes will be followed by the letter 'n'.

Abdel Khalek Sarwat Pasha, 109, 116n
Abdel Malek, Anwar, 93, 96n
Abidjan symposium, 26, 27, 32
abi-Talib, Aly ibn, 58
Adenauer, Konrad, 82
administration, confused with management, 88–9
agriculture, need for reform (Egypt), 70
Ahrar Dustoureyeen, 113
Al Hayat (Arabic-language newspaper), 6n
al Khattab, Omar ibn, 132, 144n
al Manfalouty, Mustafa Lutfi, 109, 116n
al-Aqqad, Abbas, 8–9, 109, 116n
Al-Azhar University, 94
Alexander the Great, 10
Al-Ghazali, Abu Hamid Muhammad (Hujjat al-Islam), 8, 100
'Ali, Mohamed, 42–3, 44, 103
Ali Mustafa Musharrafa, 96
Al-Jazeera TV channel, 2
Amin, Ahmed, 109
Amin, Mustapha, 115
Ancient Egyptians, 130
Ancient Greece: mathematics, origins, 35; philosophers of, 12
Arab League, 2
Arab-Israeli conflict, 3
Aristotle, 35, 57
'art of work', 83, 85
Asian Tigers, 64, 76n, 79–80
Ataturk, Kamal, 76n
autocracies, 62

backwardness, 58, 94
Baha' El Din, Ahmed, 115
ballot box, misuse, 61–2
Baring, Sir Evelyn, 43
Belarus, 19
'Benchmark', 78, 95
Bishay, Adel, 82, 96n
Bismarck, Otto von, 10, 14n
Bolsheviks, 10
Bonaparte, Napoleon, 10, 11, 14n
Breasted, James Henry, 12, 36
Brest-Litovsk Treaty (1918), 11
British Broadcasting Corporation (BBC), 110–11
Bush, President George H.W., 5n

Cairo, American University in, 102
Camp David peace agreement, 33n, 96n
Carlyle, Thomas, 12
Central Security Forces, Egypt, 70–1
Chiang Kai-shek, 16
China: civilization, 12, 118, 135–6; ethnic community, 118; People's Republic of, 25; teamwork, 140–1
Churchill, Winston, 17
'civil servant' mentality, 83
civilization/civilizations, 7–13; ancient, 135–6; characteristics, 35; definitions, 7; destiny, 11–12; education as major achievement, 4–5; human input, 8–11; values, 36; *see also* civilized march of mankind
civilized march of mankind: achievements, 12–13; hurdles impeding, 22–32; progress as outcome of, 34–41
The Clash of Civilizations (Huntington), 132
Clinton, President Bill, 17
Cold War (1945–90), 15–21; consequences, 17–21; Korea, division of, 19–21; rise of, 15–17; US policy, 27; US supremacy, 17–19
collective work (teamwork), 136–41
Columbia University, US East Coast, 102
'Comecon' (Council for Mutual Economic Assistance), 16
command economies, 88
The Conditions of the Working Class in England (Engels), 23
conspiracy theory, 2, 39–40
corruption, 38
'cowboy culture', 13
criticism, and self-criticism, 132–4
Cuba, 19
culture, individual, 127–8

Darwinism, social, 37, 38
Darwish, Sayed, 109
de Gaulle, President Charles, 95
delegation, at work, 143
Deming, W. Edwards, 128
democracy: constituting, 62; Egyptian experiment with, 47; in England, 48; established democracies, 95; human rights, consolidation, 62–3; importance of, 18; misuse of 'ballot', 61–2; models, 63; and pluralism, 118, 130–2; relative superiority of, 48; specificity of democratic process, 64; and Third World, 59, 60; truth about, 58–64; and US foreign policy, 47
destiny, 11–12
Dialectical Materialists, 9